TED SHUTTLESWORTH

The Camels Are Coming

Introduction to the
Gifts of the Spirit
Volume 1

Unless otherwise indicated, all Scripture quotations are from the King James Version of the Bible.

The Camels Are Coming: Volume 1 Introduction to the Gifts of the Spirit
ISBN 978-0-9987856-1-5

Copyright © 2021 by Ted Shuttlesworth Evangelistic Association, Inc.

All rights reserved. Content and/or cover may not be reproduced in whole or in part or in any form without the express written consent of the publisher.

www.tedshuttlesworth.com

Published by T.S.E.A., Inc.
Post Office Box 7
Farmington, West Virginia 26571
USA

Printed in the United States of America

Prophecy given to Lester Sumrall by Smith Wigglesworth in 1939

"I see the last day revival that's going to usher in the precious fruit of the earth. It will be the greatest revival this world has ever seen! It's going to be a wave of the gifts of the Spirit. The ministry gifts will be flowing on this Planet Earth. I see hospitals being emptied out, and they will bring the sick to churches where they allow the Holy Ghost to move."

Contents

Foreword	vii
Introduction	xi
The Camels Are Coming	1
The Four Bodies of Christ	22
Now Concerning Spiritual Gifts: Their Existence	60
Now Concerning Spiritual Gifts: Their Divisions	76
Now Concerning Spiritual Gifts: Their Administrations & Operations	90
Now Concerning Spiritual Gifts: Their Purpose	113
Now Concerning Spiritual Gifts: Their Divine Nature	131

Foreword

Statistics seem to indicate that we're living in a generation that's not interested in church or religion. Some have even labeled it a "post-Christian" society.

One research group discovered that many young people who have grown up in church are making the choice to leave when they become adults. However, they've left out an important piece of information—the *kinds* of churches the young people are leaving—*dead ones*.

I don't blame them. I'd leave, too. Who could possibly be satisfied with dead, dry religion. These churches are the fulfillment of the Apostle Paul's prophecy to Timothy. They have a form of godliness but deny its power.

After traveling all over the world, I can assure you that no matter their age, race, or economic status, anyone who encounters the true power of God is interested in it and hungry for it. This is not a new religion or modified orthodoxy; it's book-of-Acts-style Christianity.

Lester Sumrall once referred to the church as "Acts 29." Interestingly, the book describing the Acts of the Apostles gives us twenty-eight chapters of narrative and finishes with no formal ending.

Dr. Sumrall taught that the reason the book of Acts has no formal conclusion is because the power of God working through the church continues to this day.

The gifts of the Spirit are the tools God gave us to accomplish His plan on the earth. Jesus was sent to *"destroy the works of the devil"* (1 John 3:8). We have been empowered by the Holy Spirit to do the same works Christ did.

Many have forgotten that the reason God sent the Holy Spirit to the church was so we could receive power to produce evidence to the world (Acts 1:8).

As Nigerian pastor, Bishop David Oyedepo, once said, "If your faith has no proof, it's fake." Throughout the early church, God confirmed His Word with signs that followed it. We should still see those signs today.

These gifts of the Spirit point people back to Jesus. As John wrote, *"Many believed in [Jesus] name when they saw the signs that he was doing"* (John 2:23).

For as long as I can remember, I've watched my father proficiently operate in all nine gifts of the Spirit. The Lord has used him to demonstrate the power of God for over forty years.

Many signs, wonders, and miracles have marked the revival meetings in which he has ministered. These supernatural moments have always brought people to a saving knowledge of Jesus Christ.

I believe this point is an important one. I've always been uneasy about those who seem to manifest spiritual gifts but have no redemptive value. Someone may be able to supernaturally recite your bank card number, but to what end? What does it accomplish?

I've seen my father have words of knowledge about what brand of cigarettes someone smokes. The end result, however, is deliverance from addiction.

Whenever Jesus or the early Christians manifested the gifts of the Spirit, it brought about a redemptive result—salvation, healing, Holy Spirit baptism, deliverance, etc.

As you read this book, may God give you a fresh hunger and desire for the gifts of the Spirit. May you step out by faith to bring help to a hurting world. Get ready for a new adventure of faith.

Ted Shuttlesworth Jr.

Introduction

My son has encouraged me to take what I have learned about the moving of the Spirit and the subsequent gifts of the Spirit and release this series as a teaching for this generation.

The years that have gone by have increased my desire for the things of the Spirit. My earliest memories are of the move of God in the churches that my Mom and Dad pastored. My father was also a campmeeting and revivalist preacher in his Pentecostal fellowship. He would take us to these meetings where the Spirit of God moved. Whether the setting was a tent, or the old, wooden tabernacles, there was an atmosphere of expectancy that filled the air.

Our church was different — the people sang loudly and with feeling. The sounds of revival got down in my soul and the lively music and shouts of God's people set my heart for Christ forever. We were different from the ordinary and the

Lord performed the extraordinary.

My father's preaching was fiery and Christ-centered. My mother played the piano, and the altars brought repentance, great miracles of healing, and the outpouring of the Spirit.

There was one more thing that made us different. We spoke in tongues, and that began my fascination with the gifts of the Spirit. The atmosphere would be charged with the Spirit. We were Pentecostal!

A new era was born with the coming of the Holy Spirit. A divine energy was released on the Earth and in every believer who received the promise of the Father.

Jesus encouraged his followers to wait for the outpouring of the Spirit and what would happen to them when the Spirit came upon them.

> **And, being assembled together with them, commanded them that they should not depart from Jerusalem, but wait for the PROMISE OF THE FATHER, which, saith he, ye have heard of me.**
>
> **Acts 1:4**

> **But ye shall receive power, after that the Holy Ghost is come upon you:**
>
> **Acts 1:8**

I love the way that Carl Brumback, a Pentecostal author and minister from the 1940s, described the outpouring of the Holy Spirit on the day of Pentecost. The following passage is an excerpt from *What Meaneth This*, a book that contained transcripts of his radio messages on the subject of the Holy Spirit:

> Jerusalem was happy. The great Feast of Pentecost with its memories of Sinai and its thanksgiving for the wheat harvest was at hand. Devout men, out of every nation under heaven were wending their way once again toward their beloved Zion. They were coming to worship at her temple and to pay her homage. — The pilgrims were singing as they came, and their sweet songs brought great joy to Jerusalem. Her children were rising up from the north and the south, the east and the west, and calling her blessed! Hear, O Israel! I was glad when they said unto me; Let us go into the house of the Lord.[1]

God's plan was to pour out His Spirit when the Jews from around the world would come to Jerusalem. What a divine moment of destiny! Christ had been crucified and then rose from the dead. Jerusalem's attention was focused on what had happened, and this was the backdrop for the coming of the Holy Spirit on the day of Pentecost.

120 believers gathered and waited for the promise.

---

1. Brumback, Carl. *What Meaneth This*. Gospel Pub House, 1947. Print

> And when the day of Pentecost was fully come, they were all with one accord in one place. And suddenly there came a sound from heaven as of a rushing mighty wind, and it filled all the house where they were sitting. And there appeared unto them cloven tongues like as of fire, and it sat upon each of them. And they were all filled with the Holy Ghost, and began to speak with other tongues, as the Spirit gave them utterance.
>
> **Acts 2:1-4**

We are commanded to receive the Holy Spirit by Jesus Himself, so this is not optional but an essential part of every believer's walk of faith. God's plan to empower His creation began in the garden in Eden with the promise of a Redeemer.

> And I will put enmity between thee and the woman, and between thy seed and her seed; it shall bruise thy head, and thou shalt bruise his heel.
>
> **Genesis 3:15**

Revelation is progressive. John the Baptist said, *"There cometh one mightier than I after me,"* (Mark 1:7.) Christ was revealed as the Mighty One. Then, Jesus encouraged His disciples with these words, *"And I will pray the Father, and he shall give you another Comforter that he may abide with you forever;"* (John 14:16.)

The revelation continued. The Apostle Paul helped the early Christians in Ephesus understand this progression when he taught them:

> **Have ye received the Holy Ghost since ye believed? And they said unto him, we have not so much as heard whether there be any Holy Ghost. And he said unto them, unto what then were ye baptized? And they said, Unto John's baptism. Then said Paul, John verily baptized with the baptism of repentance, saying unto the people, that they should believe on him which should come after him, that is, on Christ Jesus. When they heard this, they were baptized in the name of the Lord Jesus. And when Paul had laid his hands upon them, the Holy Ghost came on them; and they spake with tongues, and prophesied.**
>
> **Acts 19:2-6**

The mighty baptism of the Holy Spirit and His subsequent gifts have inspired me. They have drawn me down a path of desire that caused me to study the Bible and be filled with the Spirit and, yes, yield to the Holy Spirit and operate in these precious gifts.

I have taken my notes and messages of over forty-five years of seeking the Lord and compiled them into these studies for a generation that has arisen who may not know of the precious move of the Spirit. I have written this book for you that *"Follow after charity, and desire spiritual gifts,"* (1 Corinthians 14:1.)

Ted Shuttlesworth Sr.
Hill Cottage, West Virginia
February, 2021

CHAPTER 1
The Camels Are Coming

The gifts of the Holy Spirit are both sacred and anointed. They are sacred because of their holy origin, and anointed because God empowers them to bless humanity. They are a part of God's plan for the total redemption of man.

The Apostle Paul defines what a man is in his letter to the Thessalonian church:

> **And the very God of peace sanctify you wholly; and I pray God your whole SPIRIT and SOUL and BODY be preserved blameless unto the coming of our Lord Jesus Christ.**
> **1 Thessalonians 5:23**

Oral Roberts called it "the whole gospel for the whole man." It's man on three dimensions: spirit, soul, and body.

Are you ready for an adventure of faith? There is a journey that will take you from the ordinary to the extraordinary, and from the natural realm to the glorious world of God's power and presence. The Old Testament contains many wonderful stories of faith and redemption that give us insight regarding how God deals with His children.

God having provided some better thing for us, that they without us should not be made perfect.

Hebrews 11:40

Now all these things happened unto them for examples: and they are written for our admonition, upon whom the ends of the world are come.

1 Corinthians 10:11

ABRAHAM: THE FATHER OF FAITH

So then they which be of faith are blessed with faithful Abraham.

Galatians 3:9

In our studies on these precious gifts of the Spirit, the life of Abraham must be examined. The Apostle Paul's writings to the churches in Rome and Galatia show us the importance of Abraham and how the gifts of the Spirit operate.

The Apostle Paul reveals to us the connection between the patriarch Abraham and the gifts of the Spirit:

> **He therefore that MINISTERETH to you the Spirit, and WORKETH MIRACLES among you, doeth he it by the works of the law, or by the hearing of faith? Even as ABRAHAM believed God, and it was accounted to him for righteousness. Know ye therefore that they which are of faith, the same are the children of Abraham.**
>
> **Galatians 3:5-7**

So we that desire to operate in the gifts must follow the faith of Abraham because *"He therefore that ministereth"* and works *"miracles"* operates *"even as Abraham believed God."*

We see that the *"differences of administration"* (1 Corinthians 12:5) and in particular the *"working of miracles"* (1 Corinthians 12:10) operate by the hearing of faith. Our example for this kind of faith is the life of Abraham.

THE TOWER OF PRIDE

We are introduced to Abraham after God confounded the languages of men at a plain in Shinar. It was later referred to as Babel. The people had decided that they would build a tower reaching into the heavens. Their pride was the sin that the Lord judged.

> And they said one to another, Go to, let us make brick, and burn them thoroughly. And they had brick for stone, and slime had they for mortar. And they said, Go to, let us build us a city and a tower, whose top may reach unto heaven; and LET US MAKE US A NAME, lest we be scattered abroad upon the face of the whole earth.
>
> Genesis 11:3, 4

It's interesting to note that they were building with counterfeit materials using, *"brick for stone"* and *"slime for mortar."*

Those who would seek to make a name for themselves are in for a fall. We are reminded that this spirit has its roots in Satan's desire to do the same.

> How art thou fallen from heaven, O Lucifer, son of the morning! how art thou cut down to the ground, which didst weaken the nations! For thou hast said in thine heart, I will ascend into heaven; I will exalt my throne above the stars of God: I will sit also upon the mount of the congregation, in the sides of the north: I will ascend above the heights of the clouds; I will be like the most High.
>
> Isaiah 14:12-14

It is this "counterfeit" that the devil tries to use to lead men and women away from the Lord.

Remember that God's plan is always based on redemption. His plan is to restore fallen man.

The devil's plan is based on opposition. His desire is to steal, kill, and destroy the work of God (John 10:10).

Man's plan is based on deception. A man without Christ has fallen into sin and is subject to pride for in the flesh there *"dwelleth no good thing"* (Romans 7:18).

> **PRIDE goeth before destruction, and an haughty spirit before a fall.**
> **Proverbs 16:18**

What was the one thing that the devil wanted but could never have? We see the will of the devil revealed in Isaiah chapter 14 when he said five times, *"I will."* God is the I AM which is the reason Lucifer said *"I will"* — because he isn't. God said *"Let us make man in our image, after our likeness"* (Genesis 1:26).

The one thing the devil wanted to be (like the most-high God) is the thing God created us to be. Every time the devil sees you, it reminds him of what he can never be. That is why he seeks to destroy the image of God in mankind by sicknesses and diseases, wars and famines, and destructions and calamities.

Yet, our great God has provided us the gifts of the Spirit to redeem fallen man and restore us to our rightful place in Him.

THE JAMAICAN WITCH DOCTOR

I was ministering on the island of Jamaica in 1975. The Lord led me there from a vision I received at the altar of a youth camp in western Pennsylvania.

During one service, an altar call was given and the evangelist said, "God is calling a young man into the ministry tonight." I felt that he was speaking to me, so I got up and went to the altar where I fell on my knees and surrendered to that call. The Lord gave me a vision. In that vision, I saw myself preaching and everywhere I looked, the people were black.

I thought God was calling me to be a missionary to the continent of Africa. There are times when God shows us things and we put our own interpretation on them. That's what I did that night.

Seven years later, I was standing on a wooden platform in Kingston, Jamaica. Looking across that scene of beautiful black people, I realized that was the vision that I had seen seven years before!

Do you know what a wonderful feeling it is to know that you're in the perfect will of God? That night, I knew that I had not missed God's calling on my life — not even by an inch.

Suddenly, out of the crowd, came a man who held a stick with bones hanging attached by strings to the top. He was trying to put a spell on me. He began to growl at me and shake the bones on his stick.

I ran and jumped off of the platform landing right in front of the witch doctor and stood face to face with him. I felt the *gift of faith* flow through my spirit, and before he could do anything else, I shouted in his face.

His eyes grew wide, he dropped his stick, turned around, and ran off of the field.

I later found out that there were many Jamaicans being controlled by this witch doctor. His power was the *counterfeit*, but the gifts of the Spirit in operation that night demonstrated the real power of God and hundreds were saved in that meeting.

Here is a lesson that I have learned: *you can be in God's perfect will and working for Him, but that doesn't mean that the devil will not try to hinder you.*

1. ABRAHAM'S BODY

There are three experiences in the life of Abraham that show us how God made him righteous.

> **For what saith the scripture? Abraham believed God, and it was counted unto him for righteousness.**
> **Romans 4:3**

These three experiences are his call which represents his flesh being submitted to God's will (Genesis 12:1), his offering to Melchizedek speaks of the offering that he gave by an act of his will (Genesis 14), finally, his communion with God represents God's dealing with his spirit through his intercession for Lot's family (Genesis 18).

Notice, God worked from the outside in. He dealt with Abraham's body, soul, and spirit. It is after the work of the cross that God deals with us spirit, soul, and body. (1 Thessalonians 5:23) God changes us from the inside out.

Abraham's call represents the physical separation of his flesh from the Ur of the Chaldees. We understand that the flesh wars against the spirit:

> **For the flesh lusteth against the Spirit, and the Spirit against the flesh: and these are contrary the one to the other: so that ye cannot do the things that ye would.**
> **Galatians 5:17**

If Abraham was to receive the promise, he had to leave the land where the curse began. Mesopotamia was where the Garden in Eden was located. It was here that the first Adam opened the door for Satan's deception to come in.

Mesopotamia was also the land of the red clay. That land was called "Adamah." The Bible says that God called their name Adam (Genesis 5:2).

The Scripture reminds us *"My spirit shall not always strive with man; for that he also is FLESH."* (Genesis 6:3) Just as Mesopotamia was the land where the curse came, God was taking Abraham to the land of promise where the blessing would come. The curse is not greater than the blessing and it cannot keep you from God's best.

> **Now the Lord had said unto Abram, Get thee out of THY COUNTRY, and from thy kindred, and from thy father's house, unto A LAND THAT I WILL SHEW THEE:**
> **Genesis 12:1**

God's desire has always been to make Himself known to man. That story is seen from the first book to the last book of the Bible. In Genesis 3:9, He walked in the garden in the cool of the day and called to His man Adam, *"Where are you?"*

Then, in the book of Revelation, we see Christ standing at the door and knocking. He promised to those who would hear His voice that He would come in and fellowship with them (Revelation 3:20).

There is a gap in the life of Abraham from when the Lord first called him until He made a covenant with Abraham. The Bible gives us these interesting words that indicate there may have been a season between Abraham's call and the covenant the Lord made with him. *"Now the Lord HAD SAID unto Abram,* (Genesis 12:1)

Remember, he was raised in an environment where many gods played a part in his religious training. It was this spirit of idolatry into which Abraham was born.

> Even Terah, the father of Abraham, and the father of Nachor: and they served other gods.
>
> Joshua 24:2

That is exactly what the Apostle Paul warned us about when he wrote by the Holy Spirit: *"Ye know that ye were Gentiles, carried away unto these dumb idols, even as ye were led"* (1 Corinthians 12:2). So then, you cannot operate in the gifts of the Spirit until you are led out of sin into the glorious light of Jesus Christ.

Now, Abram is confronted with the fact that there is one God and *that* God now wants him to leave his family, country, and even his religious mindset and go to a place of which he had no knowledge. The Spirit always leads us into a place of blessing.

> By faith Abraham, when he was called to go out into a place which he should after receive for an inheritance, OBEYED; and he went out, not knowing whither he went. By faith he sojourned in the land of promise, as in a strange country, dwelling in tabernacles with Isaac and Jacob, the heirs with him of the same promise: for he looked for a city which hath foundations, whose builder and maker is God.
>
> Hebrews 11:8-10

I have taught people for years that obedience is the key to prosperity. We must do what God tells us to do without hesitation. The Bible shows us that, *"And Abram was very rich in cattle, in silver, and in gold"* (Genesis 13:2).

What wonderful faith he had. He gave up what he knew for that which he did not know. He was looking for a city that was not built yet. He left for a place he did not know. He obeyed God. That is how the gifts operate in the life of a believer. The *utterance* gifts help us speak things that we don't know. The *power* gifts help us attempt things that we can't do. The *revelation* gifts help us see what God sees.

Abram had not yet left the Ur of the Chaldees and the last place he came to was Haran. Eventually, Terah died there. So we see that Abram's last experience before he left was the death of Terah.

If you are not willing to die to self-will and desires in order to follow the Lord, then you will never enter into the promise. Even Jesus had to die and go to a different world so that the Holy Spirit and His gifts of promise could come to you and me. The Apostle Paul reminds us:

> **For to me to live is Christ, and to die is gain.**
> **Philippians 1:21**

The gifts of the Holy Spirit come by promise. To be used of God, you must surrender your will to Him. God then made a covenant with Abram that blessed two worlds.

> And I will make of thee a great nation, and I will bless thee, and make thy name great; and thou shalt be a blessing: And I will bless them that bless thee, and curse him that curseth thee: and in thee shall all families of the earth be blessed.
>
> Genesis 12:2, 3

Later, we learn that this became the foundation of faith for the church, as well.

> And the scripture, foreseeing that God would justify the heathen through faith, preached before the gospel unto Abraham, saying, In thee shall all nations be blessed. So then they which be of faith are blessed with faithful Abraham.
>
> Galatians 3:8, 9

Oh, the great care of God for His church! He sent His best to confirm His Word with signs following. The gifts of the Spirit represent God's highest and best for the church who is united with Christ. God cares for you!

2. ABRAHAM'S SOUL

> And Melchizedek king of Salem brought forth bread and wine: and he was the priest

> **of the most high God And he blessed him, and said, Blessed be Abram of the most high God, possessor of heaven and earth: And blessed be the most high God, which hath delivered thine enemies into thy hand. And he gave him tithes of all.**
>
> **Genesis 14:18-20**

One of the greatest acts of your will is to give to God. It takes faith to give an offering. Abraham, the father of our faith, taught us that in this walk of faith there is a time to give God an offering.

When we yield our will to God, He then gives us the manifestation of His will which is the Law of Seedtime and Harvest.

> **"For I know the plans I have for you," declares the Lord, "plans to prosper you and not to harm you, plans to give you hope and a future."**
>
> **Jeremiah 29:11 NIV**

It is then that we see Abraham begin to build altars where he offered sacrifices to God.

> **And he removed from thence unto a mountain on the east of Bethel, and pitched his tent, having Bethel on the west, and Hai on the east: and there he builded an altar unto**

> the Lord, and called upon the name of the Lord.
>
> Genesis 12:8

Now we see Abraham willing to give an offering unto God. This first altar was between Bethel and Hai. Bethel means "the house of God." Hai means "a heap of ruins."

Somewhere between a ruined life and the presence of God there must be an altar. It is at that point in your life where you confess.

> **No man can say that Jesus is the Lord, but by the Holy Ghost.**
>
> 1 Corinthians 12:3

Abraham set the example for us by his confession that we, too, will be able to operate in the gifts of the Spirit as we surrender our will to the will of God.

3. ABRAHAM'S SPIRIT

> **And the Lord appeared unto him in the plains of Mamre: and he sat in the tent door in the heat of the day;**
>
> Genesis 18:1

The understanding of the gifts of the Spirit is birthed out of prayer. We see this in the third phase of Abraham's life. The Apostle Paul taught us that prayer is a spiritual exercise.

What is it then? I will PRAY with the spirit, and I will PRAY with the understanding also:
                                                        1 Corinthians 14:15

When Abraham left the Ur of the Chaldees, he began a walk of faith in his *flesh*. When Abraham gave an offering to Melchizedek, it was an act of his *will* (or soul which is your mind, will and emotions). Now, the day came that Abraham prayed to God out of his *spirit*.

The Lord revealed to Abraham that destruction was going to come to Sodom. Many years ago my wife and I stood on the field where Sodom and Gomorrah were destroyed. There were burnt, black rocks everywhere.

When the Lord told Abraham of the coming judgment upon Sodom, the Bible says that *"Abraham stood yet before the Lord"* (Genesis 18:22). It reminds us of the Scripture where God looked for a man to stand in the gap (Ezekiel 22:30).

Abraham prayed and asked God to spare Sodom. He started with fifty souls then asked God if He'd spare the city for forty-five, forty, thirty, twenty, and finally ten souls. Afterward, the Lord departed from Abraham.

The city was destroyed and I've always wondered if Abraham stopped praying too soon. What if he had asked for one because Lot was living there?

The gifts of the Spirit are for one and everyone. Since the Apostle Paul said that the faith of Abraham brought the operation of the gifts of the Spirit *"by the hearing of faith even as*

Abraham believed God" (Galatians 3:5,6).

The gifts of the Spirit are God's guarantee that *"all nations be blessed"* (Galatians 3:8).

THE CAMELS ARE COMING

Look at the covenant that God made with Abraham:

> **And I will bless them that bless thee, and curse him that curseth thee: and in thee shall all families of the earth be blessed.**
> **Genesis 12:3**

The Ur of the Chaldees was Abraham's original home. Ur was the capital of the ancient Chaldean empire in Mesopotamia. God called Abraham out of the Ur of the Chaldees and made a covenant with him. There was only one challenge: he had no heir. Who can be used in the gifts of the Spirit?

> **For the promise is unto you, and to your CHILDREN, and to all that are afar off, even as many as the Lord our God shall call.**
> **Acts 2:39**

The walk of faith produces the manifestation of God's promises. The day came when God gave Abraham his son of promise—Isaac.

> And God said, Sarah thy wife shall bear thee a son indeed; and thou shalt call his name Isaac: and I will establish my covenant with him for an everlasting covenant, and with his seed after him.
>
> **Genesis 17:19**

Since the Apostle Paul has shown us that the gifts of the Spirit work because of Abraham, the father of our faith (Galatians 3:5-7), we can see the work of the Holy Spirit in this story. The supernatural power of God is seen throughout the Bible from Genesis that begins with the words *"In the beginning, God,"* to the final words of the Revelation of Jesus Christ, *"the Grace of our Lord Jesus Christ be with you all. Amen."*

This story reveals to us how God uses the Holy Spirit and the gifts of the Spirit to redeem fallen man.

Abraham represents God our Father.

Isaac represents Christ our Savior.

If the blessings of Abraham are ours, then the same requirements that God gave to Abraham would also apply to us.

==You cannot be used of God and do what you want to do and expect God to bless it.==

King David knew this:

> The Lord is my shepherd; I shall not want. He maketh me to lie down in green pastures: he LEADETH me beside the still waters. He restoreth my soul: he LEADETH

me in the paths of righteousness for his name's sake.

Psalm 23:1-3

Obedience, then, is following the leading of the Lord. You have this promise from God:

For as many as are LED by the Spirit of God, they are the sons of God.

Romans 8:14

The day came when God led Abraham to take his son and offer him up as a sacrifice. The Bible says that this was a test by God for Abraham's faith. God never tests you with evil, but God always tests us with good.

Every GOOD gift and every perfect gift is from above, and cometh down from the Father of lights, with whom is no variableness, neither shadow of turning.

James 1:17

When Isaac saw the wood and the fire, his question was, *"where is the lamb?"* (Genesis 22:7) Abraham's reply is why you and I will see Jesus someday. *"God will provide himself a lamb"* (Genesis 22:8).

The revelation of who God is and what He can do is progressive as we continue to *"walk by faith and not by sight"* (2

Corinthians 5:7).

Abraham found out that God was Jehovah Jireh. When Abraham offered up his only son, God reconfirmed His covenant with Abraham, but He added one more blessing. *"Thy seed shall possess the gate of his enemies"* (Genesis 22:17).

Isaac represents Jesus Christ who is the only begotten Son of the Father. Christ is seen as the Lamb of God. When Jesus went down to the waters of Jordan at Bethabara, John the Baptist saw Him coming and said, *"Behold the Lamb of God, which taketh away the sin of the world"* (John 1:29). What a beautiful story of redemption.

Then, the day came that Isaac was to take a bride. The church is the Bride of Christ.

> **And I John saw the holy city, new Jerusalem, coming down from God out of heaven, prepared as a BRIDE adorned for her husband.**
> **Revelation 21:2**

Abraham enlisted the help of his servant Eliezer to go and bring back a bride for his son.

> **And the servant took ten camels of the camels of his master, and departed; for all the goods of his master were in his hand: and he arose, and went to Mesopotamia, unto the city of Nahor.**
> **Genesis 24:10**

Eliezer represents the Holy Spirit. He climbed upon the lead camel as they did in those days. Following Eliezer were nine camels loaded down with precious gifts. These gifts are to be given to the bride.

Eliezer's instruction was to give these gifts to the daughter that was coming to draw water from the wells in the evening.

Rebekah, who represents the church, comes to the well to fulfill the prophetic act that Eliezer asked of the Lord:

> **And let it come to pass, that the damsel to whom I shall say, Let down thy pitcher, I pray thee, that I may drink; and she shall say, Drink, and I will give thy camels drink also: let the same be she that thou hast appointed for thy servant Isaac; and thereby shall I know that thou hast shewed kindness unto my master.**
>
> **Genesis 24:14**

Rebekah comes out and begins to water the camels.

> **Christ also loved the church, and gave himself for it; That he might sanctify and cleanse it with the washing of water by the word,**
>
> **Ephesians 5:25-26**

The power of redemption's story is seen in this Old Testament example. Our Father, who is God, gave us Jesus Christ who has made us *"heirs of Salvation"* (Hebrews 1:14). The Holy Spirit was sent to bring a bride back to Heaven.

We need to understand that it takes the gifts of the Holy Spirit to separate the church from the world, and it takes the same gifts to bring the church back to the Father in Heaven.

There must be a "watering" (or teaching) about the gifts so that they may be manifested for the church to receive and operate in them. Once those gifts are received, then the powerful union with Christ takes place.

God is working in the final evening of time to bless and prepare the church. Time is running out. Our story finishes with the Christ standing and waiting for His Bride. The Holy Spirit and His gifts are moving us towards our final home.

> **And Isaac went out to meditate in the field at the eventide: and he lifted up his eyes, and saw, and, behold, THE CAMELS WERE COMING.**
>
> **Genesis 24:63**

CHAPTER 2

The Four Bodies Of Christ

When the church was born on the Day of Pentecost, God began a new era on the earth to accomplish His purpose. He poured out His Spirit upon all flesh (Joel 2:28). The Baptism of the Holy Spirit and the manifestations and demonstrations of the Spirit are God working through us and with us.

> **For I have received of the Lord that which also I delivered unto you, that the Lord Jesus the same night in which he was betrayed took bread: And when he had given thanks, he brake it, and said, Take, eat: this is my body, which is broken for you: this do in remembrance of me.**
> **1 Corinthians 11:23-24**

The Apostle Paul starts his introduction to the gifts of the Spirit immediately after his teaching on the meaning of the Lord's Table.

I believe that this is significant because it is more important that we are in close communion with Christ than it is to be used in the spiritual gifts.

They both are important, but our relationship with Christ is the most important and vital thing. The ability to operate in the gifts of the Spirit comes from this relationship.

There are many who have sought to be used in the gifts but have never sought Christ. However, if we are in contact with the Giver of the gifts then those gifts should operate as well.

The writer inspired by the Holy Spirit further says;

> **For he that eateth and drinketh unworthily, eateth and drinketh damnation to himself, NOT DISCERNING THE LORD'S BODY. For this cause many are weak and sickly among you, and many sleep.**
> **1 Corinthians 11:29, 30**

It is this lack of understanding about the body of Christ that keeps the *gift of healing* from operating. As a result, many of God's children battle infirmities and sicknesses and there are those who die before their time.

Here we see the *gifts of healing*, which is one of the nine gifts of the Holy Spirit, is hindered in its operation because of the lack of understanding of who Jesus is and what He has done.

> **Now concerning spiritual gifts, brethren, I would not have you ignorant.**
>
> 1 Corinthians 12:1

This is why you must *"Study to shew thyself approved unto God, a workman that needeth not to be ashamed, rightly dividing the word of truth"* (2 Timothy 2:15).

You cannot operate in the gifts of the Spirit and be used by God without the knowledge of what they are and how they operate. The mighty Baptism of the Holy Spirit and the manifestation and demonstration of the gifts of the Spirit are not optional.

I believe many fall short of God's best and His perfect will because they have become content to live without these gifts of the Spirit in operation in their lives.

The gifts flow out of the operation of the Holy Spirit and are a direct result of the nature of God being made manifest through the believer.

Three *gifts* help us to *act* like God. They are the gifts of power — The *gift of faith*, the *working of miracles*, and the *gift of healing*.

Three *gifts* help us to *think* like God. These are the gifts of revelation — the *discerning of spirits*, the *word of knowledge*, and the *word of wisdom*.

Three *gifts* help us to *speak* like God. These are the gifts of utterance — *tongues*, the *interpretation of tongues*, and *prophecy*.

> **What? know ye not that your body is the temple of the Holy Ghost which is in you, which ye have of God, and ye are not your own?**
>
> **1 Corinthians 6:19**

We are compared to the Temple of God. The Temple was fashioned into three parts: The Outer Court, the Inner Court which is the Holy Place, and the Holy of Holies (Exodus 27).

The Tabernacle or Temple illustrates man in three dimensions (1 Thessalonians 5:23). Our bodies are the *Outer Court* which touches both the natural world and the supernatural realm.

Our soul is the *Inner Court* and this is where the lampstand (Zechariah 4) and the table of shewbread (Exodus 25) were placed. It is our mind, will, and emotions.

Our Spirit is like the *Holy of Holies*, the dwelling place of God's Spirit. What once was dead in trespasses and sin, is now brand new.

All three of God's redemptive works are operating for the whole man. Salvation is for your spirit, the Baptism of the Holy Spirit is for your soul, divine healing is for your body. Therefore, there are three redemptive experiences that God has provided for every man and woman.

The gifts of the Spirit always operate in a redemptive

context. The utterance gifts flow out of your *spirit* which is the hidden man of the heart. (1 Peter 4:3) The revelation gifts give us the *Mind* of Christ for our minds. The power gifts operate for the strength and healing of your *body*.

> **My son, attend to my words; incline thine ear unto my sayings. Let them not depart from thine eyes; keep them in the midst of thine heart. For they are life unto those that find them, and health to all their flesh.**
> **Proverbs 4:20-22**

The Spirit of man is the real man. We are spirits that have a soul and live in a body. The gifts of the Holy Spirit can be released by God's Word. The writer of Proverbs shows us that life and health come from what we hear, what we see, and how we think.

Our approach to these gifts comes through the Lord's Table. The two elements of communion are the wine and the bread. The blood covenant of the cross brought full deliverance from the dominion of sin and gave us the fellowship of the Holy Spirit.

The Old Testament priests understood that once the blood was applied, the oil was to come next. (Leviticus 14:16,17,28,29)

Here is a guideline for those who desire to operate in the gifts of the Spirit. The blood and then the oil upon the ear signifies the *hearing of faith*. That is why the Holy Spirit inspired the writer of Proverbs to write *"incline thine ear."*

> **So then FAITH cometh by hearing, and hearing by the word of God.**
> **Romans 10:17**

Then, the blood and oil applied to the thumb represent *faith in action*. The man with the withered hand in Mark chapter 3 received the *working of miracles* when Jesus said *"stretch forth thine hand."*

The blood and oil upon the right toe speaks of the *walk of faith*. We understand that *"we walk by faith and not by sight."* (2 Corinthians 5:7)

All of the operations of the gifts come by faith operating in your heart, and at best we only operate by the measure of faith that we have.

> **For I say, through the grace given unto me, to every man that is among you, not to think of himself more highly than he ought to think; but to think soberly, according as God hath dealt to every man the MEASURE OF FAITH.**
> **Romans 12:3**

That is why the Bible calls them gifts. They're not earned, or given because of your skills, intelligence, or abilities. They are gifts. This explains why Paul said:

> For we know in PART, and we prophesy in PART. For now we SEE through a glass, darkly; but then face to face: now I know in part; but then shall I know even as also I am known.
>
> 1 Corinthians 13:9,12

Here we have three ways that the gifts can operate — and I have found that this is how they operate in my ministry. Sometimes, I just speak it and while I am speaking, God gives me more to say. Sometimes, I just know it and many times that knowing has come to me in prayer. Then, there are times that I can see it.

GOD GAVE ME GIFTS ON MY BIRTHDAY

In one service years ago, I was praying and fasting for the meeting. This was in the beginning of God using me in the gifts of the Spirit. The Lord spoke to me in my room that day and said

"I'm going to show you what I want to do in the service tonight. These are the four songs that should be sung to create the atmosphere in which I will move.

Then, as you look out on the right side there will be a man who is deaf. After you pray for him there will be a girl in front of him who has tumors and is scheduled for an operation. After you pray for her, there will be a woman on the back row. She was in the laundromat today and asked me to heal her during this meeting."

One of the reasons that I was praying and fasting was that it was my birthday and I wanted God to use me in a greater way in the days ahead.

I went to the service that night filled with expectation. The service began, and although I did not tell him, the song leader sang the first three songs that I had on my list God had given me. He did not lead us in the fourth song, so I took the microphone and led the congregation in singing it. Then, I preached the Word God gave me. When I was done, I looked to my right and I saw a man sitting on the fifth row.

"Sir, God's going to heal you of deafness," I said.

"What?!" He shouted. The people all laughed. I prayed for him and the Lord opened his deaf ears.

Then, I turned and saw a young girl sitting in front of him. I asked her to stand and told her that God has shown me that she had fibroid tumors and was scheduled for surgery. She began weeping. I laid my hands upon her head and she began to rejoice as she felt the pain go out of her body.

Then, I went back up on the platform so I could see the whole crowd. I pointed to my left and said, "There is a woman sitting on the back row and you were in the laundromat today and asked the Lord to heal you. Come up here and I'll pray and the Lord will heal you."

When she stood in front of me, I knew her condition was diabetes.

"You asked the Lord to heal you of diabetes today," I said. I'll never forget her response.

"Yes, yes!" She cried. I laid my hands on her and later that week she testified that her sugar levels were normal.

The gifts of the Spirit are like headlights on a car. The further you go, the more you can see.

I believe that we have settled for less of God when we need to have more of God. The communion table represents our relationship with Jesus Christ. Whatever we receive comes from Him. Only Christ had the Spirit without measure.

> **For he whom God hath sent speaketh the words of God: for God giveth not THE SPIRIT BY MEASURE unto him.**
> **John 3:34**

We operate by the Spirit *in measure* (Romans 12:3). However, our measure can be increased. Where you are now in God is not where you're going to finish. Your faith can grow. There are different levels of faith.

We see that there are those who have *no faith*.

> **And he said unto them, Why are ye so fearful? how is it that ye have NO FAITH?**
> **Mark 4:40**

Then we see there are those who have *little faith*. Jesus addressed Peter as he was walking on the water and began to sink:

> And immediately Jesus stretched forth his hand, and caught him, and said unto him, O thou of LITTLE FAITH, wherefore didst thou doubt?
>
> Matthew 14:31

Then, there were two people in Scripture who had *great faith* according to Christ. The first was a centurion who came to Christ for the healing of his servant. After seeing the centurion's understanding of His power, Jesus said to him:

> "Verily I say unto you, I have not found so GREAT FAITH, no, not in Israel."
>
> Matthew 8:10

The second example is found in the story of a woman who came to Christ whose daughter was being tormented by a demon.

> Then Jesus answered and said unto her, O woman, GREAT IS THY FAITH: be it unto thee even as thou wilt. And her daughter was made whole from that very hour.
>
> Matthew 15:28

My heart is moved when I think of the truth that Jesus is presently working with us today. No matter where your faith is, He is willing to give you even more. Perhaps this is why the communion table reminds us that it is *"as oft as you drink it"* (1 Corinthians 11:25).

When you continue to exercise, you build your strength and stamina. Our faith that overcomes the world (1 John 5:4).

When Jesus said *"Have faith in God,"* I believe it was because our faith can come to an end. Like those disciples when fear attacked them, they found themselves with no faith. There is a great difference between our faith and the faith of God. There is a substance to that faith.

Now faith is the SUBSTANCE of things hoped for, the evidence of things not seen.
Hebrews 11:1

When the woman with the issue of blood touched Christ's garment, what flowed into her body? (Mark 5:27-30)

What got into the cloths and aprons that Paul prayed over and sent from his body that healed the sick and caused demons to be cast out? (Acts 19:12)

What was in the bones of the prophet that caused the dead soldier to be resurrected when his dead body touched the prophet's grave? (2 Kings 13:21)

What does the Bible mean when it says *"the eternal weight of glory?"* (2 Corinthians 4:17)

The Scripture shows us that faith can grow, faith has a substance to it, and faith can be imparted to those who position themselves to receive. My life's verse is:

> But without faith it is impossible to please him: for he that cometh to God must believe that he is, and that he is a rewarder of them that diligently seek him.
>
> Hebrews 11:6

The reward of faith comes from the blessed communion table which gives us access by faith to the body of Christ — the element that saves and heals all mankind.

1. CHRIST'S FLESH AND BLOOD BODY

> Take, eat: THIS IS MY BODY, which is broken for you: this do in remembrance of me.
>
> 1 Corinthians 11:24

The two elements of the communion table are the wine and the bread which speak of Christ's natural body which was flesh and blood.

We see that Christ had a *flesh and blood body*. He came into this world as a man to take us back to Heaven.

> Behold, a virgin shall be with child, and shall bring forth a son, and they shall call his name Emmanuel, which being interpreted is, God with us.
>
> Matthew 1:23

Christ was God in the flesh and He came to set man free from the power and dominion of the devil. One of the operations of the gifts is the *discerning of spirits*. When Christ came, the devil did not know who he was:

> **Which none of the princes of this world knew: for had they known it, they would not have crucified the Lord of glory.**
>
> **1 Corinthians 2:8**

But Jesus knew who the devil was. We see, then, that the devil is limited in his knowledge. The devil doesn't know our thoughts. He only knows what we say. John reveals the purpose of Christ coming to the Earth:

> **For this purpose the Son of God was manifested, that he might destroy the works of the devil.**
>
> **1 John 3:8**

From the time of Jesus' baptism in the Holy Spirit, the anointing of the Holy Spirit and the gifts of the Spirit were being manifested to undo the works of evil which came upon every one of us through the first Adam's sin.

> **The first man is of the earth, earthy; the second man is the Lord from heaven.**
>
> **1 Corinthians 15:47**

When Adam ate of the forbidden fruit, he lost the dominion that God had given him and sin and death entered into the world (Romans 5:12).

Christ entered into the desert and *did not eat* and regained the dominion that the first Adam lost. When He came out of the time of being tested, the Bible says He *"returned in the power of the Spirit"* (Luke 4:14). If you desire to be used with God's power, you will be tested.

The first miracle of Jesus was when He turned the water into wine (John 2). Later, the devil tried to use water to kill Jesus. A great storm arose when Jesus and the disciples were headed to the country of the Gadarenes. The disciples became fearful and woke Jesus up.

> **And he arose, and rebuked the wind, and said unto the sea, Peace, be still. And the wind ceased, and there was a great calm.**
>
> **Mark 4:39**

Notice that the Bible says He *"rebuked"* the wind, but He *"spoke"* to the sea. The word translated rebuke is the same word found in Mark 9:25 when *"He rebuked the foul spirit."*

This means there was a devil in the wind causing the great storm. Yet, Jesus didn't rebuke the sea. He said, *"Peace, be still."* That's because His Father made the sea and Jesus wouldn't have rebuked His Father.

The water, which Jesus used for the miracle at the wedding, was the element that the devil tried to use on the sea of Galilee to destroy the miracle worker. But, the Greater One was in the boat and not in the storm. So we can see that even Jesus was tested along these lines.

I have noticed that when I preach about certain things in the Scripture, I am tested in those same areas.

The Apostle Paul, to whom the Lord gave the revelation of these gifts of the Spirit, found himself dealing with a buffeting spirit sent from Satan. In my mind, no message has been harder fought than the Pentecostal message.

Why is it that the devil fights against this message? The answer can be found in Acts chapter 10.

> **How God anointed Jesus of Nazareth with the Holy Ghost and with power: who went about doing good, and healing all that were oppressed of the devil; for God was with him.**
>
> **Acts 10:38**

The anointing of the Holy Spirit destroys every work of the devil. *The gifts of the Spirit are both tools and weapons that the Lord uses.* We see that by His own example.

It has been said that the gifts of the Holy Spirit are what the stone was to David and what the jawbone was to Samson as they destroyed God's enemies.

If we do not have the gifts of the Spirit in operation, we will go from one defeat to another. However, God wants us to live in victory, not to be caught up in the struggles of life.

Then he answered and spake unto me, saying, This is the word of the Lord unto Zerubbabel, saying, Not by might, nor by power, but BY MY SPIRIT, saith the Lord of hosts.

Zechariah 4:6

When Jesus ministered upon the earth, He declared, *"The Spirit of the Lord is upon me"* (Luke 4:18). This means that our natural bodies, created in the image of God, can have the mighty Spirit of God upon us and within us. I believe that this is what Paul meant when he told Timothy:

Wherefore I put thee in remembrance that thou STIR UP THE GIFT OF GOD, which is in thee by the putting on of my hands.

2 Timothy 1:6

In the Old Testament, Nehemiah had the desire to rebuild the fallen walls of Jerusalem. Jerusalem speaks of God's holy habitation. He returned with the children of Israel to accomplish this work.

Every one with one of his hands wrought in the work, and with the other hand held a weapon.

Nehemiah 4:17

The gifts of the Spirit help us to take back what the devil has stolen. They are seen as tools. For example, praying in the Spirit allows us to build up our most holy faith (Jude 20). This is how we can be built up in our natural man by the operation of the gifts of the Holy Spirit.

The gifts of the Spirit are also weapons of our warfare as we work to destroy the strongholds of the devil. Paul reminded Timothy:

> **This charge I commit unto thee, son Timothy, according to the prophecies which went before on thee, that thou by them mightest war a good warfare;**
>
> **1 Timothy 1:18**

Years ago, I was holding a meeting in Salem, New Jersey. The Lord put it in my heart to stay at the church through the night until the morning. I had preached that Sunday morning and night, but sensed that something needed to be broken through.

I started by praying in English, and I prayed for everything I could think of. When I looked at my wristwatch, it wasn't even midnight. I had worn myself out in my natural body.

Then, the Lord led me to pray in tongues and even prophesy about what I expected Him to do in the meeting.

Friend, I don't know if you've ever had this happen to you, but the next six hours flew by as if it were just a few minutes. I took a bottle of oil, anointed every seat, and asked God to bring the people in to fill them.

I anointed every window and door in the sanctuary and asked God to put angels around the building.

I anointed the pulpit where I would preach and I even anointed the communion table on the floor in front of the pulpit.

Then, I took the oil and poured it on my head and asked God to anoint me.

When Monday night came, the power of God filled that auditorium. The Holy Ghost became the preacher that night. When I finished with the Word, I called a girl to come down to the altar. She had come into the service on crutches.

That night, I felt as bold as a lion. I took the crutches from the girl and asked the ushers to hold her by the arms. I took her crutches and broke them over the altar and said to the girl, "Now God has to heal you!"

Suddenly, the girl broke loose and took off running around the church healed of a broken leg. The people stood and gave God praise.

The word spread throughout the Eastern Shore. The next night, a reporter from Dover came and wrote an article. Wednesday morning it was front-page news!

The crowds came from all around that region and the Lord filled all of the pews that I'd anointed with oil.

A local radio station came and asked if they could air the services live and I laughed when they put the transmitting equipment underneath the communion table.

It was the gifts of the Spirit that broke this region open to the gospel of Jesus Christ. Multiplied hundreds came and were saved, and healed as a result of praying in tongues and seeing the *working of miracles* operate.

> **Through mighty signs and wonders, by the power of the Spirit of God; so that from Jerusalem, and round about unto Illyricum, I have fully preached the gospel of Christ.**
> **Romans 15:19**

Here we see that the gifts of the Spirit in operation through mighty signs and wonders expand the area of ministry.

Where you begin in faith is not where you'll finish in *the things of the spirit*. The Kingdom of God is based upon increase. Be encouraged and don't give up.

When I was a boy, my father had us sit down and watch a live speech by Winston Churchill given in a university in the mid-western part of the United States. It was considered to be one of his greatest speeches and it consisted of three words: "Never, never quit!"

The operation of the gifts of the Spirit multiply the scope of your ministry!

When Jesus ministered, the Bible says that His *"fame went abroad into all that land"* (Matthew 9:26).

When He returned from the desert until He went to the cross, Jesus was healing the sick, casting out devils, raising the dead, and cleansing the lepers. He accomplished this as a man in a flesh and blood body.

> **Verily, verily, I say unto you, He that believeth on me, THE WORKS THAT I DO SHALL HE DO ALSO; and greater works than these shall he do; because I go unto my Father.**
> **John 14:12**

We identify with Christ. He is our master example. Never allow fear of failure to keep you from fulfilling the will of God for your life. You, too, can walk upon the earth and follow the footsteps of Jesus to see your generation set free as the gifts of the Spirit flow out of you to bless our world. Praise God forevermore!

2. CHRIST'S FLESH AND BONE BODY

We are living in the last days. There are two parallel moves taking place in the spirit realm. One move is the promised outpouring of the Holy Spirit. This great outpouring was prophesied by Joel, Peter, and James.

> **And it shall come to pass afterward, that I will pour out my spirit upon all flesh; and your sons and your daughters shall prophesy, your old men shall dream dreams, your**

young men shall see visions:

> Joel 2:28

And it shall come to pass in the last days, saith God, I will pour out of my Spirit upon all flesh: and your sons and your daughters shall prophesy, and your young men shall see visions, and your old men shall dream dreams:

> Acts 2:17

Be ye also patient; stablish your hearts: for the coming of the Lord draweth nigh.

> James 5:8

One of the nine gifts of the Spirit that is seen in operation in the last days is the *gift of prophecy*. The outpouring of the Holy Spirit on the Day of Pentecost filled believers and they began to speak with other tongues (Acts 2:4). So we see that the gifts of the Spirit are a part of the last-day manifestation of the Spirit in and through every believer.

The Bible also tells us that in the last days evil will grow worse (2 Timothy 3:13). The devil will fight against this move of the Holy Spirit with great anger. He will do everything that he can through an increase of demonic power in a way that this world has never seen.

> **Therefore rejoice, ye heavens, and ye that dwell in them. Woe to the inhabiters of the earth and of the sea! for the devil is come down unto you, HAVING GREAT WRATH, because he knoweth that he hath but a short time.**
>
> Revelation 12:12

Time is running out for souls that live on planet Earth. It is the mighty gifts of the Spirit in operation that hinder the enemy's plans.

I believe that the one who is restraining the power of evil and iniquity in 2 Thessalonians 2:7 is the Holy Spirit Himself and that the second body of Christ represented by flesh and bone gives us a picture of our authority.

What is missing in this second part of Christ's body if not *His blood!* The blood of Jesus was formed by God the Father in the womb of the Virgin Mary. When Christ was born, He was the first man created since Adam whose blood had no sin in it. Speaking of Jesus, Peter wrote:

> **Who did no sin, neither was guile found in his mouth:**
>
> 1 Peter 2:22

It was that sinless blood shed on the cross that caused man to regain dominion and authority. We must become spiritual forensic examiners and trace the blood that Jesus gave to see what was accomplished which brought the outpouring of the Holy Spirit to defeat the wrath of Satan in these last days.

The first evidence was when they beat Him with a whip and placed stripes on His back. (John 19:1; Mark 15:15) The day that the stripes were laid upon Christ's back, tearing the flesh and bloodying our Savior, was the day that the power of sickness and disease was broken off of all mankind. Isaiah prophesied:

> **But he was wounded for our transgressions, he was bruised for our iniquities: the chastisement of our peace was upon him; and WITH HIS STRIPES WE ARE HEALED.**
> **Isaiah 53:5**

The power of the blood of Jesus is seen in this transition from a flesh and blood body to His flesh and bone body. Quoting the Prophet Isaiah, Matthew wrote in His Gospel: *"Himself took our infirmities, and bare our sicknesses"* (Matthew 8:17). The Apostle Peter, looking back at the cross, said:

> **Who his own self bare our sins in his own body on the tree, that we, being dead to sins, should live unto righteousness: by whose stripes ye WERE HEALED.**
> **1 Peter 2:24**

I call this the *past tense* of healing. All that God is ever going to do to heal you was accomplished on the cross over 2,000 years ago.

The second evidence was when they made a crown out of thorns and placed it upon Christ's head. They beat His head with a reed.

Years ago, I attended a one-room school house in Western Pennsylvania. Just a small building with a stove in the center of the room and a cloak room where we hung our coats and put our bags of lunch. We drank the water from a pump outside.

One day, one of the students stole another boy's lunch. Our teacher kept cut branches that you would be whipped with if you broke the rules. If they did that today, they would go to jail. However, this was a common practice in those days.

When the teacher had the boy bend over the desk she asked him to take his coat off. When he did, we saw that he had no shirt on! You could see his ribs and he looked as if he had not eaten in days. We all felt bad for him and another boy jumped up and said, "Let me take his whipping for him!"

This is what Jesus did for us so that we could be free from Satan's power. The crown of thorns speaks of God filling the gap. Jesus took our place.

The story of Job tells us of how the devil sought to destroy this servant of God. One of the things that the devil recognized was that there was a *hedge of protection* around the life of Job.

> **Hast not thou made an HEDGE about him, and about his house, and about all that he hath on every side?**
>
> **Job 1:10**

You must understand that the devil did not break the hedge. Job broke it through fear.

> **For the thing which I GREATLY FEARED is come upon me, and that which I was afraid of is come unto me.**
>
> **Job 3:25**

Ecclesiastes 10:8 tell us, "*He that diggeth a pit shall fall into it; and whoso breaketh an hedge, a serpent shall bite him.*"

The crown of thorns that was placed upon Christ's head was the acacia thorn which was common to the land the Bible refers to as Uz.

We could say that the crown of thorns that Jesus wore represents the rebuilding of God's hedge of protection around you and your family, and in this final hour, the enemy will not harm you fulfilling the words of Jesus:

> **Behold, I give unto you power to tread on serpents and scorpions, and over all the power of the enemy: and NOTHING SHALL BY ANY MEANS HURT YOU.**
>
> **Luke 10:19**

Now we look with eyes of faith to the hill called Golgotha. Three crosses are outlined by that darkening sky.

It is the Man on the middle cross that our eyes of faith see. There is blood streaming from His head, from His beaten back, and the wounds in His hands and feet.

A Roman soldier steps up with a spear in his hand. My friend, there was still some blood left, but sin demanded full payment.

The First Adam sold us out on the auction block of sin, but the Last Adam bought us back with His blood.

> **Forasmuch as ye know that ye were not redeemed with corruptible things, as silver and gold, from your vain conversation received by tradition from your fathers; But with the PRECIOUS BLOOD OF CHRIST, as of a lamb without blemish and without spot:**
> **1 Peter 1:18-19**

I was preaching in the northeastern part of America in a state that bordered Canada. A fellowship of churches sponsored me to come and preach in a high school every night for a week.

I was staying on the American side of the border and I had no money. I was believing that the offering they gave me at the end of the week would help me get home.

There was a McDonald's at an exit on the American side

that I passed by every night. I could smell the food through the vents in my car. I decided I would pull in and get a cup of water.

I went into the counter and I asked for some water. However, the girl brought out a tray with hamburgers, french fries, and a drink.

"You made a mistake," I said. "I didn't order this."

The manager walked over and said, "Hello, Brother Shuttlesworth." When he said it, I smelled a blessing coming my way. He took a red pen from his pocket and wrote *paid in full* on the bill.

"I'm going to preach this all over the world," I said. Jesus paid for what I needed when I couldn't, and He signed it with His precious, red blood.

It turned out that this man had gotten saved in the meetings that week. The Lord knows what you need.

The last of Christ's blood was shed when the soldier thrust the spear in His side. How powerful and how precious was that moment.

> **But one of the soldiers with a spear pierced his side, and forthwith came there out BLOOD AND WATER.**
>
> **John 19:34**

That blood poured into the ground which had been cursed since Adam had fallen. I personally believe that Christ's blood, shed that day, reversed the curse of Genesis

3:15. Now Christ's body was just flesh and bone for all of His blood had been emptied out. The writer of Hebrews tells us that:

> **Forasmuch then as the children are partakers of flesh and blood, he also himself likewise took part of the same; that through death he might destroy him that had the power of death, that is, the devil; And deliver them who through fear of death were all their lifetime subject to bondage.**
> **Hebrews 2:14-15**

The *crown of thorns* restored dominion and authority to man.

The *stripes on Christ's back* brought healing and deliverance.

The *blood from His wounded side* brought salvation to all humanity.

> **How much more shall the BLOOD OF CHRIST, who through the eternal Spirit offered himself without spot to God, purge your conscience from dead works to serve the living God?**
> **Hebrews 9:14**

One of the things that has helped me to operate in the

gifts of the Spirit and especially the *gift of faith* is when I meditate on what Jesus did. I believe that this is a fundamental teaching that we might be free from every work of the enemy.

The day He stood in the garden before Mary, His body was just flesh and bone. His blood was offered up upon the altar on the mercy seat in Heaven. (See Hebrews chapter 9.)

Jesus said to her, *"Touch me not; for I am not yet ascended to my Father"* (John 20:17).

The question has been asked, *"What happened between the cross and the throne?"*

The scriptures say that Christ descended that we might ascend (Ephesians 4:10). He went down into the very bowels of the earth and confronted Satan in his dark domain.

The scriptures tell us that He took the vesture, or the authority, in which Satan trusted. He took the keys of death, hell, and the grave (Revelation 1:18), and He ascended up on high.

3. CHRIST'S GLORIFIED BODY

Now that Jesus' blood has been accepted by God the Father, we see that there was a transition between His appearance to Mary in the garden, where He told her *not* to touch Him because he had not yet ascended to the Father, to the day He appeared to the disciples in a closed room by coming through the walls and instructing Thomas *to* touch Him.

> Then the same day at evening, being the first day of the week, when the doors were shut where the disciples were assembled for fear of the Jews, came Jesus and stood in the midst, and saith unto them, Peace be unto you.
>
> John 20:19

Here we see that the natural realm cannot withstand the supernatural realm. The glorified body of Jesus represents the superiority of the Lord of Glory. This helps us understand the Scripture:

> But the natural man receiveth not the things of the Spirit of God: for they are foolishness unto him: neither can he know them, because they are spiritually discerned
>
> 1 Corinthians 2:14

All revelation knowledge flows from Christ to the believer because of this transformation. Our bodies will never be in Heaven. They will come to an end upon the earth even as Christ's natural body did. However, He received a glorified body when He ascended up on high and this is the same hope for every believer.

> But we all, with open face beholding as in a glass the glory of the Lord, are CHANGED

INTO THE SAME IMAGE from glory to glory, even as by the Spirit of the Lord.
                              2 Corinthians 3:18

One day, we will receive our glorified bodies. In that hour, when we are absent from the body and present with the Lord, there will be a great change that takes place for us.

When John saw Jesus on the isle of Patmos, the continued glory, that the disciples saw in the closed room, had made even more of a change as John described Christ's appearance.

And in the midst of the seven candlesticks one like unto the Son of man, clothed with a garment down to the foot, and girt about the paps with a golden girdle. His head and his hairs were white like wool, as white as snow; and his eyes were as a flame of fire; And his feet like unto fine brass, as if they burned in a furnace; and his voice as the sound of many waters. And he had in his right hand seven stars: and out of his mouth went a sharp twoedged sword: and his countenance was as the sun shineth in his strength.
                              Revelation 1:13-16

We are reminded of the time when Moses came down from the mountain and his face shone with the glory of

God. God's children could not even look upon him because of that bright glory that was upon Moses.

Paul writes in 2 Corinthians chapter 3:

> **But if the ministration of death, written and engraven in stones, was glorious, so that the children of Israel could not stedfastly behold the face of Moses for THE GLORY of his countenance; which glory was to be done away: How shall not the ministration of the spirit be rather glorious?**
>
> **2 Corinthians 3:8,9**

The glory that was upon Moses' face had to pass away. Why? I believe it was that a greater glory would take its place. *This is how the ministry of the Holy Spirit works.*

The gifts of the Spirit were given to bring us to the place where the glory of God outshines the darkness of this world.

When I traveled with Brother Schambach, many times I heard him tell the story of how God healed a boy with twenty-six diseases. Brother Schambach worked with evangelist A.A. Allen in the 1950s. They were holding a crusade in the Fairground Auditorium in Birmingham, Alabama.

He told us, "God opened the veil and let me see into the future." A woman from Tennessee drove to the crusade with her friend. She brought her little, four-year-old boy who needed twenty-six miracles.

Brother Schambach preached faith in the day services, then

gave out prayer cards for those who needed prayer. Brother Allen would call out the cards at night and pray for the people.

She came to Brother Schambach and said, "I am running out of money. I only have $20 left." She had been staying at a motel, eating in diners, and giving offerings in every meeting. Brother Allen had not called her card, and she was upset. She did not want to leave without Brother Allen praying for her boy. Brother Schambach said, "I will personally take your child to the man of God's trailer if he does not pray for your child tonight."

That night, Brother Allen bounced out on the stage and said, "I am going to receive an offering of faith." Brother Schambach said that he had never heard those words before. The people looked puzzled and Brother Allen explained. "An offering of faith is when you give God something you can't afford to give. If you give what you think you can afford, there is no faith in it."

When the people came down to give, Brother Schambach saw that woman come and put something in the bucket. He jumped off the platform and looked into the bucket and there was her $20 bill. He said he went behind the platform and wept. The woman's faith stirred him

He came back out and heard Brother Allen say, "I am being carried away in the Spirit. I see a large white building." Brother Schambach said that he was a little hardened to it because he had seen Brother Allen do this before; it was how God used him.

Then Brother Allen said, "I hear babies crying. There

are twelve doctors standing around a baby. That baby has twenty-six diseases. They are saying the child will not even live to be one year old. Now I see a woman leaving Knoxville in a Ford. She is crossing the Tennessee/Alabama border and driving on the grounds. That child is here tonight. Bring him down here. Tonight, God is going to give him twenty-six miracles!" Brother Schambach told us that he shouted, "Tonight is that baby's night!"

The child had many problems. He had no male organs, was blind, deaf, dumb, his tongue hung out of his mouth and lay on his chin. His arms and legs were twisted and his elbows were attached to his tummy. His knees touched the elbows, and he had clubfeet. His spine was twisted and he had lung and heart trouble.

Brother Allen asked everyone to bow their heads and pray, but Brother Schambach said, "I kept my eyes open." When Brother Allen started walking with the child, Schambach followed him.

Suddenly, the tongue snapped like a rubber band back into his mouth. The two eyes were covered with a white milky substance and started swirling like whirlpools, and two blue eyes appeared. Both arms and legs snapped free, and his clubfeet straightened and became normal.

Then, like a sergeant, the Spirit moved on the twelve wheelchairs to the left. The crippled folks in them all stood up at the same time! Then, like a maestro conducting an orchestra, the crowd's eyes went to the right side of the tent where the stretchers were, and everyone stood up completely healed. People started streaming down the aisles and threw hearing aids, glasses, canes, crutches, and walkers on the platform. Women lost weight as tumors disappeared from their bodies!

Brother Schambach prophesied that no man will take glory for what God is going to do in this last move. He encouraged us that in the last days the body of Christ would be healed and no one would be sick. He said, "God opened the veil and let me see into the future."

I believe the day is coming when the body of Christ will step into this greater glory and the gifts of the Spirit will remove all sicknesses and diseases from the church, and we will have the testimony:

> **That he might present it to himself a GLORIOUS CHURCH, not having spot, or wrinkle, or any such thing; but that it should be holy and without blemish.**
> **Ephesians 5:27**

4. CHRIST'S ETERNAL BODY

> **Now ye are the body of Christ, and members in particular.**
> **1 Corinthians 12:27**

The church is the body of Christ, past, present, and future. Christ is seen as the Head of that body.

> And hath put all things under his feet, and gave him to be THE HEAD over all things to the church, Which is his body, the fulness of him that filleth all in all.
>
> Ephesians 1:22,23

After the Apostle Paul teaches us about the gifts of the Spirit, he then speaks of the body of Christ. Our understanding of the body of Christ, which is the church, is critical to the operation of these gifts of the Spirit.

> For as the body is ONE, and hath many members, and all the members of that one body, being many, are one body: so also is Christ.
>
> 1 Corinthians 12:12

The devil knows that if he can bring division and break down that one body, then the gifts of the Spirit will not operate as God has intended them to do. Divisions strengthen the carnal flesh, but unity brings the power of God into operation. The carnal man cannot receive from God.

> For whereas there is among you . . . DIVISIONS, are ye not carnal, and walk as men?
>
> 1 Corinthians 3:3

Years ago, I went to hear a minister preach. He told a story to those gathered about the importance of treating each other right and walking in love towards each other. He came out of a meeting in Dallas, Texas that he attended with other ministers. One of those ministers was a great evangelist that God was using to bring signs and wonders to the world. Our brother related this story:

> When I looked at the man getting into his car, the Lord spoke to me and said, *"Go tell that man that he needs to judge himself in three areas or his life will be shortened. Tell him to judge himself in his weight. Tell him to judge himself in the way he handles money. Tell him to judge himself in the way he treats other ministers of the Gospel."*

As I started to walk toward him, other ministers gathered around him and I never delivered that word to him.

Sometime later, my wife and I attended a Voice of Healing convention at Angelus Temple in Los Angeles, California. The host of the convention stood and told us, "Word has just come in that the evangelist had been rushed to the hospital." He then invited the crowd to pray for the man.

When I stood to go down to the altar to pray, the Lord said to me, *"It's too late. He did not judge himself."*

Then the word came to my wife and I that he had passed away.

The Apostle Paul instructed us by the Spirit of God that every member of the body of Christ is important. No one in Christ's body is more important than another. It is the love of God that binds us all together as one.

> **Now ye are the body of Christ, and members in particular.**
> **1 Corinthians 12:27**

After this teaching about the fourth body of Christ, there comes the Apostle Paul's teaching on the gifts of the Spirit.

> **And God hath set some in the church, first apostles, secondarily prophets, thirdly teachers, after that MIRACLES, then GIFTS OF HEALINGS, helps, governments, DIVERSITIES OF TONGUES.**
> **1 Corinthians 12:28**

Our understanding of this teaching determines the manifestation of the gifts of the Spirit. It is our desire to see God move in this final hour. How important is it, then, that we understand that we need to judge ourselves?

> **For if we would judge ourselves, we should not be judged.**
> **1 Corinthians 11:31**

CHAPTER 3

Now Concerning Spiritual Gifts: Their Existence

> Now concerning spiritual gifts, brethren, I would not have you ignorant.
>
> 1 Corinthians 12:1

Paul ends any and all speculation as to the existence of Spiritual gifts with this one phrase: *"concerning spiritual gifts."* There are spiritual gifts. There are those who are opposed to the Pentecostal experience and argue that there is no biblical proof of the existence of the manifestations of spiritual gifts today. Paul says, *"There are spiritual gifts."*

God has always had someone ready to step in and keep the light of the gospel shining brightly in every age. The Pentecostal message has endured from the Day of Pentecost until this present day. Church history shows us that when the lamp of God was growing dim and almost out, then He would raise up a people who would *"contend for the faith which was once delivered unto the saints."* (Jude 1:3)

ERE THE LAMP OF GOD WENT OUT IN THE TEMPLE

The Old Testament story of Samuel illustrates this constant battle of the flesh warring against the spirit. Eli's father was a priest called by God to minister to the children of Israel when they were in Goshen. He lived in Pharaoh's house. Later, Eli became the priest in Israel. He came out of Egypt to answer the call of God but Egypt never fully came out of him.

The Lord was angered with him because he allowed his two sons to become worshippers of Belial. Their evil broke the promised blessing that the Lord had given to Eli.

> **Wherefore the Lord God of Israel saith, I said indeed that thy house, and the house of thy father, should walk before me forever: but now the Lord saith, Be it far from me; for them that honor me I will honor, and they that despise me shall be lightly esteemed.**
>
> **1 Samuel 2:30**

Here we see that some of God's promises are conditional. When you honor God, He will honor you. If not, then you cannot have His blessing. The day came when the news of the death of his sons was brought to him. Eli then heard that the ark of God was taken and he fell backward and broke his neck and died. The Spirit gives us the word "heavy" which speaks of his flesh. (1 Samuel 4:18) The flesh always wars against the spirit. This goes back to the time of the Edomites who were a constant enemy to the children of Israel. The Edomites were the people from the region of Adamah which means "the red clay."

They were representative of the flesh warring against the children of Israel who represent the Spirit. The Bible says, *"no good thing dwells in the flesh."* (Romans 7:18)

Eli gave more attention to his flesh than the lamp of God which was in the Holy Place. He was allowing the lamp to go out because he was more concerned about his flesh than he was about the *things of the Spirit.*

One of the reasons why the gifts of the Spirit are not in operation as they should be in the church, is because the church has not been paying attention to spiritual things as she should, and has become content to remain in ignorance of these Spiritual gifts. Even though there is some light, they have not followed Paul's admonition when he wrote:

> **But covet earnestly the best gifts: and yet shew I unto you a more excellent way.**
> **1 Corinthians 12:31**

Eli's attention to prosperity and the desire for natural

things caused him to become fat.

> "Wherefore kick ye at my sacrifice and at mine offering, which I have commanded in my habitation; and honor thy sons above me, to make yourselves FAT with the chief of all the offerings of Israel my people?"
>
> 1 Samuel 2:29

Eli used the people's offerings for the Lord to become "fat." He neglected his sons although God had promised that his lineage would serve the Lord as priests. God's promise and favor lifted off of Eli and his house. The Lord bypassed Eli and his sons and called young Samuel as His priest and prophet. The fire kept burning!

Many times, the church forgets the One who gave them their blessings to begin with.

We are reminded of the "lukewarm" condition of the church of Laodicea. Their condition was a result of what Jesus said to the Apostle John.

> Because thou sayest, I am RICH, and INCREASED WITH GOODS, and HAVE NEED OF NOTHING; and knowest not that thou art wretched, and miserable, and poor, and blind, and naked:
>
> Revelation 3:17

So we see that their lukewarm condition came from their focus on prosperity. There is nothing wrong with prosperity. In fact, the Apostle Paul said that the operation of the gifts of the Spirit causes us to *"profit withal."* One translation reads, *"to become successful."*

In the last few years, I have had to believe God for millions of dollars to preach on television, the great outdoor crusades, the publication of literature and materials, the building of an orphanage, the feeding of the poor, and so much more. The message is free, but costs the church something to get that message out freely.

We must prosper and God wants to bless us in a big way, but we are not to allow that blessing to take our focus off of the *light* of the Gospel. We need to keep the fire burning in our hearts for the lost, the least, and many times, the last.

ARE THE GIFTS STILL WORKING?

Some teach that tongues ceased after John — the last Apostle that walked with Christ — died (1 Corinthians 13:8) and that the gifts of the Spirit are no longer for today. Those who believe this have to ignore church history and what the Lord is doing today.

When we were in Bible school, we learned that the Lord always had a remnant that would do His will. Gordon Lindsay, a leader during the Voice of Healing years, wrote in his book *Bible Days Are Here Again*:

"There have been periods in human history when Divine Revelation was rare. After God manifested Himself to Abraham, Isaac and Jacob and his sons, there was a period of centuries when Israel heard no special word from God. Then came the Call of Moses and the Vision of the Burning Bush (Exodus 3) With mighty signs and wonders, the Lord redeemed Israel and led her out of bondage into the Promised Land.

After the miracles of Exodus, there was another lull in Divine Revelation. Speaking of this time the Scriptures declare "And the word of the Lord was precious in those days; there was no open vision." 1 Samuel 3:1 This period came abruptly to an end with the notable ministries of Samuel, David the Psalmist, and the prophets.

Following the days of the prophet Malachi, there began what has been called the 400 Silent Years – a period of Divine Silence that was not broken until the appearance of John the Baptist, and the Ministry of Our Lord Jesus Christ.

After several centuries in which the Early Church manifested a ministry marked by signs and wonders and miracles, there began a long period commonly spoken of as the Dark Ages which was characterized by an almost absence of the gifts and power of the Apostolic Church. At length, a monk by the name of Martin Luther heard from heaven and his message heralded the Great Reformation. John Wesley, John Knox, Charles G. Finney, and others received distinct messages from

God, which in effect changed the destinies of nations and altered the tide of history."[1]

I could also add that there were tongue-talking men and women that healed the sick such as the Albigenses in France during the 12th and 13th centuries. The Waldensians who sought to follow the Apostolic Creed, despite their misunderstanding of riches and their adherence to poverty, they had the gifts in operation, too.

The outpouring of the Holy Spirit in America is well documented and the saints of God called "Gift People" in New England in the years 1874-1875 received the Baptism of the Holy Spirit and spoke with tongues.[2]

My wife is from Providence, Rhode Island and it was there that R.B. Swan and his people were filled with the Holy Ghost. God moved in New England thirty-one years before the outpouring of the Spirit at Azusa Street in Los Angeles.

My wife and I knew the Jelley family, whose parents were a part of that move, as well as the Chase family. I preached for Brother Jelley's son in 1977 in Hartford Connecticut, and last saw him in Maine after he turned 100.

They had heard of the unusual move of God in England

---

1. Lindsay, Gordon. *Bible Days Are Here Again: Divine Healing for Today and Gods Plan for Ending Sickness*. G. Lindsay, 1949. 9. Print
2. Frodsham, Stanley H. *With Signs Following*. Gospel Pub. House, 1946. 10. Print

under the ministry of D. L. Moody in 1873. There is a book that tells this story entitled, *Moody and Sankey in Great Britain* by Robert Boyd. Here is that story published in part by Stanley Frodsham in the book *With Signs Following*:

> When I got to the rooms of the Y.M.C.A. I found the meeting on fire. The young men were speaking in tongues and prophesying.

After the outpouring of the Spirit at Azusa Street, the newspapers across the Nation and around the world carried the story of this unusual revival. The gifts of the Spirit were manifested but there was no teaching and very little understanding of what was happening.

I met Fred Vokrot in Lancaster, Pennsylvania in 1978. He was in his 90's and I was 23. The Lord had just begun to use me in the *gift of healing* and the *working of miracles*. That night, I cast the deaf spirits out of a man and Jesus healed him and gave him back his hearing.

Brother Vokrot motioned for me to come back and talk to him after the service.

"I saw the little green frogs," he said. I thought, *this guy is crazy*. The pastor came back and officially introduced me to Brother Vokrot.

"He is the oldest ordained minister in the Eastern District of the Assemblies of God and went to the Azusa revival with Frank Bartleman in the early days of Pentecost," the pastor told me.

After Azusa Street, another generation was raised up by God who began to teach the Pentecostal message. I am reminded of what the author of Hebrews wrote:

> **And what shall I more say? for the time would fail me to tell of Gedeon, and of Barak, and of Samson, and of Jephthae; of David also, and Samuel, and of the prophets:**
> **Hebrews 11:32**

I could paraphrase that verse to say "What more shall I say of Lester Sumrall, R.W. Schambach, T.L. Osborn, Kenneth E. Hagin, Oral Roberts, and other great men and women whom I have known and who taught me about the things of the Spirit."

HOWARD CARTER

Howard Carter was Lester Sumrall's spiritual father. He was placed in jail in Great Britain during World War I as a conscientious objector. His cell was small, dark, and damp. Water dripped down on him from the ceiling almost driving him mad.

The Lord spoke to him and said, "I am going to show you how the gifts of the Spirit operate." He felt the Lord speak to him to believe for the water to stop running down. So he said, "I command you, water, to flow the other way." And it did! The Lord spoke to him "This is the *gift of faith.*"

He wrote a book about what the Lord revealed to him in prison entitled, *Questions and Answers on the Gifts of the Spirit.*

Lester Sumrall said, "This *gift of faith* operates through the power of the Holy Spirit for the performance of supernatural exploits.

> Howard Carter, whom God has used mightily to perform spiritual exploits, once purchased by faith a church for a group of Christians. The time came for a rather large payment and he did not have a cent of it. His workers with him were troubled and in agony of prayer, but Brother Carter said, "God has assured me that I will have this full payment."
>
> At supper, the night before the final day of foreclosure on the property, the teachers in the Bible school were worried and upset. Brother Carter, on the other hand, was everything but ill at ease. He said, *"We do not need the money until tomorrow morning."* At the last mail delivery in the evening, about 9:00 P.M., a large, brown envelope was shoved into the box at the Hampstead Bible school. When Brother Carter opened it, there, in cash pounds, was the total amount necessary, and when he revealed the good news the next morning, the workers praised God and admired this spiritual gift in their leader.[1]

---

1. Sumrall, Lester. *The Weapons of Our Warfare.* Lester Sumrall Evangelistic Assn. 1960. 21. Print.

I believe that every pastor should covet this gift in building and purchasing property for the work of the Lord. You may not have the resources, but God has everything that we need.

SMITH WIGGLESWORTH

Howard Carter introduced Lester Sumrall to one of the great men of faith of that day—Smith Wigglesworth. Wigglesworth was a plumber that God called into the ministry. After he was baptized in the Holy Spirit, the Lord gave Wigglesworth a great healing ministry that touched the world.

He believed that we needed to continue to pursue the things of the Spirit. He preached this message concerning spiritual gifts, and here is a part of that transcript:

> There is a great weakness in the Church of Christ because of an awful ignorance concerning the Spirit of God and the gifts He has come to bring. God wants us to be powerful in every way because of the revelation of the knowledge of His will concerning the power and manifestation of His Spirit. He desires us to be continually hungry to receive more and more of His Spirit.
>
> God wants us to understand spiritual gifts and to "earnestly desire the best gifts." (1 Corinthians 12:31) He also wants us to enter into a "more excellent way," (1 Corinthians 12:31) which is the Fruit of the Spirit.

We must implore God for these gifts. It is a serious thing to have the Baptism and yet be stationary. We must be willing to deny ourselves everything to receive the revelation of God's Truth and to receive the fullness of the Spirit. only that will satisfy God, and nothing less must satisfy us.[1]

Smith Wigglesworth's ministry was changing the world until he passed away in 1947. The Lord used him to raise the dead, see limbs restored by creative miracles, bring hearing to the deaf, and see the lame walk.

He was known for *tongues and interpretation* and the *gift of prophecy* in the conferences that he held. He kept the fire burning.

LESTER SUMRALL

Lester Sumrall was as a missionary Evangelist and joined Howard Carter as a companion in traveling the world. He chronicled these experiences in his book *Adventuring with Christ*.

We can see how the Holy Spirit fanned the flames of revival and the gifts of the Spirit by the passing of the baton from one generation to the next.

When Howard Carter began his ministry and teaching on

---

1. Wigglesworth, Smith. *Smith Wigglesworth Devotional*. Whitaker House, 1999. 415-416. Print.

the gifts of the Spirit, there were no reference books available at the time. Howard Carter became a living epistle on the gifts of the Spirit from whom Lester Sumrall learned.

Right before World War II broke out, Lester Sumrall went to Smith Wigglesworth's house for what proved to be the last time. It was there that Wigglesworth prophesied to him:

> I see the last day revival that's going to usher in the precious fruit of the earth. It will be the greatest revival this world has ever seen! It's going to be a wave of the gifts of the Spirit. The ministry gifts will be flowing on this Planet Earth. I see hospitals being emptied out, and they will bring the sick to churches where they allow the Holy Ghost to move.

This prophecy was sent to me by Brother Sumrall's oldest son, Frank. Frank and I are a part of the generation that followed these giants in the faith.

The 1940s saw the beginning of a great, healing revival that swept the world. Entire nations were impacted by the gifts of the Spirit flowing through the ministries of Tommy Hicks, who saw the nation of Argentina brought into this revival with hundreds of thousands coming to Christ.

T.L. Osborn saw mighty revivals in many nations of the world at this time. It was said of Brother Osborn's ministry that millions of souls were swept into the Kingdom of God through his miracle ministry.

God gave him a mighty revival that ignited the island of Cuba before it fell into the hands of the Communists. Great stadiums in Cuba were filled with tens of thousands of people who came to hear the gospel and see the demonstration of God's miracle power.

T.L. Osborn told us the story of how the Jesuit Catholic priests marched against his meeting in Havana. One of those Jesuits was a young man named Fidel Castro. Always remember, the flesh wars against the spirit. The devil hates the gifts of the Spirit and has fought hard against them since the day they were first poured out.

Oral Roberts was mightily used of God to crisscross this nation under the world's largest gospel tent which held over ten thousand people. Governors of states and Presidents of the United States were impacted by his ministry. Men and women from every walk of life, who needed God's healing power after World War II, were blessed. Great joy filled this nation.

One time, Brother Roberts wrote me and told me, *"I was praying for you this morning and the Lord showed me that you're in the healing ministry with me."* It is the Holy Spirit who puts it in the hearts of His servants to pass the fire on to the next generation.

R.W. Schambach, who was like a spiritual father to me, felt the call of God to tent evangelism when A.A. Allen came to hold a crusade in Duquesne, Pennsylvania. Allen asked him to join the revival party and Brother Schambach joined him in Durham, North Carolina that fall.

Brother Schambach told me that he was always drawn to the tents. When Oral Roberts was in Harrisburg, Pennsylvania, he went forward to answer the challenge to give $100 to help launch Oral Roberts on television across America.

Brother Schambach said one of the greatest miracles he saw that gave him a desire to be used in the gifts was in a tent meeting that was conducted by Gordon Lindsay and T.L. Osborn in Harrisburg, Pennsylvania. A boxer, who was Brother Schambach's friend, had been blinded while fighting in the ring. When Brother Osborn prayed for him, Brother Schambach's buddy received his sight. Brother Schambach told me that he prayed, "Lord, use me like this."

Never forget, *desire* is born out of *demonstration*. The day came when God asked me to step up and stand on the platform of Pentecostal ministry. I was walking the streets of Chicago with a minister who turned and began to prophesy to me.

"*The Lord shows me that someday you will preach under a tent. You may even preach under the tent with R.W. Schambach. You will know men of God like Oral Roberts, Kenneth Hagin, T.L. Osborn, and Lester Sumrall, and they will help you.*"

That word of prophecy came to pass. Later, I found myself working alongside of R.W. Schambach who taught me everything I know about miracle evangelism. I met and had fellowship with each of those men of God. We ate together, rode in cars together, and sat in rooms and hotels as they told me about their journeys of faith.

Now, that torch is to be passed on to you. My natural son,

Ted, his wife Carolyn, my daughter Megan, and her husband Jonathan, are also my spiritual sons and daughters. There are others who are spiritual sons and daughters—I command every one you to receive the Holy Spirit. (John 20:22) Don't let the fire go out!

CHAPTER 4

Now Concerning Spiritual Gifts: Their Divisions

> **Now there are diversities of gifts, but the same Spirit.**
>
> **1 Corinthians 12:4**

There is a supernatural order to the gifts of the Spirit. The gifts, as listed by the Apostle Paul, can be divided into three categories.

There are three gifts that help us to THINK like God. They are the *word of wisdom*, the *word of knowledge*, and *discerning of spirits*.

There are three gifts that help us to ACT like God. They are the *gift of faith*, the *gifts of healing*, and the *working of miracles*.

There are three gifts that help us to SPEAK like God. They are *tongues*, the *interpretation of tongues*, and *prophecy*.

PETER, JAMES, & JOHN

> And after six days Jesus taketh Peter, James, and John his brother, and bringeth them up into an high mountain apart,
>
> Matthew 17:1

One of the things that the Holy Spirit shows us is that Jesus came to reveal God's divine purpose upon the Earth. Jesus taught us that:

> Jesus saith unto him, Have I been so long time with you, and yet hast thou not known me, Philip? he that hath seen me hath seen the Father; and how sayest thou then, Show us the Father? Believest thou not that I am in the Father, and the Father in me? the words that I speak unto you I speak not of myself: but the Father that dwelleth in me, he doeth the works.
>
> John 14:9-10

Jesus modeled the will of God by His actions and even by His choices. So we see that when Jesus chose Peter, James, and John from among the twelve disciples, God had a purpose for this choice. Peter is an example of the *power gifts* in action. He was the first disciple to operate in the *gift of faith*.

> **Insomuch that they brought forth the sick into the streets, and laid them on beds and couches, that at the least the shadow of Peter passing by might overshadow some of them.**
>
> **Acts 5:15**

He did not lay hands upon the sick or even anoint them with oil, but by a *gift of special faith* he believed that when his shadow would pass over the sick they would receive healing.

Later, he was delivered out of the prison by the *gift of faith*. The church prayed for Peter and God sent an angel and brought him out of the prison, and delivered him out of the hands of King Herod.

Peter was also one of the first of the disciples to operate in the *working of miracles*. We read the story in Acts chapter 3 of how Peter and John were going up to the temple to pray when the encountered a man who was lame from his mother's womb. Peter challenged that man to look at them. Then, he commanded that man in the name of Jesus Christ to rise up and walk. (Acts 3:1-6)

It was Peter who first received the revelation of how the *gifts of healing* were released by the Holy Spirit.

> **How God anointed Jesus of Nazareth with the Holy Ghost and with power: who went about doing good, and healing all that were**

oppressed of the devil; for God was with him.

Acts 10:38

When my son, Teddy, was two years old, I would bring him onto the platform and have him quote this Scripture. The reason I did this is because I think it's important to train our children in the Word and help them learn how to expect miracles from God.

Therefore, Peter represents the *power gifts*: *the gift of faith*, the *gifts of healing*, and the *working of miracles*. When Jesus called him to go the mountain, he saw the glory of God.

It's important to show the difference between the *working of miracles* and the *gifts of healing*. Mark's Gospel is considered to be the miracle book of the four Gospels. The key words for this Gospel are forthwith, immediately, and straightway. Miracles are instantaneous. The first miracle of Jesus was the turning of water into wine in John chapter 2. That took place instantly!

The second miracle of Jesus is the story of a nobleman who comes to Him on behalf of his son who is sick. He asked the Lord to heal his boy. Jesus prayed for the boy to be healed and the nobleman returned to his home:

> And as he was now going down, his servants met him, and told him, saying, Thy son liveth. Then enquired he of them the hour WHEN HE BEGAN TO AMEND. And

> they said unto him, Yesterday at the seventh hour the fever left him. So the father knew that it was at the same hour, in the which Jesus said unto him, Thy son liveth: and himself believed, and his whole house.
>
> John 4:51-53

So then, the *gifts of healing* are progressive whereas the *working of miracles* is instantaneous. The *gift of faith*, or *special faith*, is customized and works FOR you in administration whereas the *working of miracles* and the *gifts of healing* work THROUGH you in administration.

The thought is that the *gift of faith* is the only one of the nine gifts of the Spirit that works FOR you. The other eight gifts by administration work THROUGH the believer to bless others.

Jesus chose James to accompany them to the Mount of Transfiguration. James received the revelation of prayer and the importance of speaking in faith.

> But let him ask in faith, nothing wavering . . .
>
> James 1:6

James understood the power of the tongue.

> If any man among you seem to be religious, and bridleth not his tongue, but deceiveth

> **his own heart, this man's religion is vain.**
> **James 1:26**

The Lord gave him the revelation that the tongue controls our body (James 3:3). He taught us that the tongue can either produce blessing or cursing (James 3:10).

> **But the tongue can no man tame; it is an unruly evil, full of deadly poison.**
> **James 3:8**

It is interesting to me that the Lord chose to use man's tongue to release the *utterance gifts* in the earth. The sign is, the most unruly member—that last stronghold of the flesh—surrenders to the Holy Spirit and becomes the initial evidence that a man or woman is filled with the Holy Spirit.

James also operated in the *gift of prophecy*. He prophesied the end-time vision of an economic meltdown before the coming of the Lord and the encouragement to the church to be patient and rooted in faith in the last days. (James 5:1-8) So we see that the Lord gave James the understanding of the power of the tongue and the words that he prophesied are still an encouragement to us today concerning the last days.

James represents the *utterance gifts*: they are *diverse kinds of tongues*, *the interpretation of tongues*, and *prophecy*.

Our Lord also chose John to be a part of this trio. It was John who first received the revelation of *discerning of spirits*.

The first chapter of the Gospel of John reveals the manifestations of the *discerning of spirits*. The key word for revelation is the word *see*, and in the Old Testament, the prophets were considered to be *seers*.

> **(Beforetime in Israel, when a man went to enquire of God, thus he spake, Come, and let us go to the seer: for he that is now called a Prophet was beforetime called a Seer.)**
> **1 Samuel 9:9**

The first manifestation of *discerning of spirits* is to see Jesus Christ. John gives us the beginning of this revelation in John 1:34 when he records the words of John the Baptist:

> **And I SAW, and bare record that this is the Son of God.**
> **John 1:34**

Two of John the Baptist's disciples—one being Andrew, Simon Peter's brother—followed Jesus from that day forward. Andrew brought Simon Peter to see Jesus. Then, Philip, who lived in the same city as Andrew and Peter, began to follow Jesus and brought his friend, Nathanael, to the Lord. The next level of *discerning of spirits* is the discerning of a man's spirit.

> **Jesus SAW Nathanael coming to him, and saith of him, Behold an Israelite indeed,**

> in whom is no guile! Nathanael saith unto him, Whence knowest thou me? Jesus answered and said unto him, Before that Philip called thee, when thou wast under the fig tree, I SAW thee.
>
> John 1:47-48

The third level of the operation of the *discerning of spirits* has to do with angels. When the disciples were amazed that Jesus saw Nathanael when he stood under the fig tree, Jesus taught them:

> Because I said unto thee, I SAW thee under the fig tree, believest thou? thou shalt SEE greater things than these . . . verily, I say unto you, Hereafter ye shall SEE heaven open, and the angels of God ascending and descending upon the Son of man.
>
> John 1:50-51

The fourth realm of the manifestation of the *discerning of spirits* has to do with evil spirits. We need to understand that there are limits in this Gift and that the Bible says:

> For now we SEE through a glass, darkly; but then face to face: now I know in part; but then shall I know even as also I am known.
>
> 1 Corinthians 13:12

For example, when Jesus went over to the Gadarenes, a man possessed with devils came to the Lord. Jesus inquired of the devils:

> **And he asked him, WHAT IS THY NAME? And he answered, saying, My name is Legion: for we are many.**
>
> **Mark 5:9**

Although Jesus did not know the name of the devils and commanded them to tell Him their name, He was still successful in delivering the man once He confronted them by name. The name of Jesus is more powerful than any other name.

> **He raised [Christ] from the dead, and set him at his own right hand in the heavenly places, Far above . . . EVERY NAME that is named, not only in this world, but also in that which is to come:**
>
> **Ephesians 1:20-21**

We also see this limitation revealed in the ministry of the Apostle Paul. When Paul was in Macedonia, he came to a city where there was a woman who was a fortune teller that followed them around for days. She actually testified that these were great men of God.

However, the day came when Paul received this revelation and his spirit became disturbed by the woman. He turned around and commanded the demon spirit to come out of her in the name of Jesus Christ. The Bible says: *"He came out the same hour"* (Acts 16:18).

John received revelation from Jesus Christ concerning the last days. The book of Revelation contained supernatural insight concerning the condition of the seven churches in Asia Minor, judgments in Heaven, the judgments that would come upon the earth, the unveiling of the Antichrist, the Beast, the False Prophet, and the conclusion of that glorious day of the church in Heaven.

John represents the *revelation gifts*: the *word of wisdom*, the *word of knowledge*, and the *discerning of spirits*.

The *discerning of spirits* is the greatest of the three *revelation gifts*.

The *word of wisdom* reveals some future event that may affect an individual to bring about the best possible conclusion and result for that believer. It always speaks to the future.

The *word of knowledge* is a fragment of information from the mind of God concerning people, places, things, or conditions that affect a person. It reveals all these things from the past and even the present.

However, the *discerning of spirits*, as is recorded in John's Gospel, functions in all three realms of time: past, present, and future.

When Nathanael stood in front of Jesus, He saw that in the present, Nathanael was a man in whom was no guile.

He also saw by this gift that in the past, he was standing under a fig tree. Then, the Lord Jesus showed how this Gift reveals the future when He said *"ye shall see heaven open, and the angels of God ascending and descending upon the Son of man"* (John 1:51).

Because of this, the *discerning of spirits* has the greater operation of the three *revelation gifts*.

COMPANION GIFTS

I was holding a meeting in Lakeland, Florida, many years ago. One afternoon, the pastor gathered several other ministers to pray. There were about half a dozen of us, and we all found different places to kneel or sit and pray. I had been praying about how to explain to people that sometimes God uses several gifts together to bring about a demonstration of his power.

The verse of Scripture that I asked the Lord to give me revelation about was:

> **But all these worketh that one and the self-same Spirit, dividing to every man SEVERALLY as he will.**
> **1 Corinthians 12:11**

Suddenly, the pastor, not knowing what I was praying, said, "The Spirit says, 'companion gifts,' brother Ted. 'companion gifts.'"

At that moment, the Lord began to pour understanding into my heart about that verse. I saw how that sometimes God can use several gifts or operations to bring about a desired result.

We can say, then, that some of these gifts work together in ministering to the people.

When the Apostle Paul went to minister in Macedonia, he came to the city of Lystra. There was a young man who sat there and was crippled in his feet from birth. The Bible says that Paul preached the gospel there. Apparently, healing is a part of the gospel. The Apostle Paul had never been there before and the gospel had never been preached there before. However, the Scripture records these words:

> **The same heard Paul speak: who stedfastly beholding him, and PERCEIVING that he had faith to be healed, Said with a loud voice, Stand upright on thy feet. And HE LEAPED AND WALKED.**
>
> **Acts 14:9-10**

The two gifts of the Spirit that worked together were the *word of knowledge* and the *working of miracles*. When the Scripture says Paul perceived, that was the *word of knowledge*. Then, when Paul gave the command to arise and the young man jumped up, this was the operation of the *working of miracles*.

Another obvious example of companion gifts is *tongues*

and the *interpretation of tongues*. They work together.

> **I would that ye all spake with tongues but rather that ye prophesied: for greater is he that prophesieth than he that speaketh with tongues, except he interpret, that the church may receive edifying.**
>
> **1 Corinthians 14:5**

This gives us the understanding that even in the divisions of the gifts there are divisions among the operations that can also overlap.

When Paul perceived, that was one of the *revelation gifts*, but when the miracle took place, that was one of the *power gifts*. Although they were two different divisions, the Holy Spirit uses whatever is necessary to minister to us.

Tongues and interpretation of tongues are both *utterance gifts*, but one cannot function without the other if we want to bless and edify the church.

It is interesting to note that the lives of Peter, James, and John also represent the three divisions of the gifts of the Spirit. We could say that the glory came on the Mount of Transfiguration and that it had something to do with Jesus and these three disciples He chose.

These three men went up together, prayed together, and they saw the glory together. They represent the companion gifts in the Holy Spirit. I believe it was because they followed Jesus that God's glory was revealed. When they came down from the mountain, that glory from that heavenly encounter was upon them.

The gifts of the Spirit were sent by God to the Earth by the Holy Spirit so that His glory would come upon the Earth.

> **For God, who commanded the light to shine out of darkness, hath shined in our hearts, to give the light of the knowledge of the glory of God in the face of Jesus Christ.**
> **2 Corinthians 4:6**

Peter was so moved by this glory and visitation that he suggested that three tabernacles be built.

Our bodies are referred to as the temple of the Holy Ghost and that the gifts of the Spirit are for the profit of our spirit, souls, and body (1 Corinthians 6:19).

These three divisions can be defined in a broad sense as the manifestation of the nature of God restoring man to the supernatural plan of redemption.

The *power gifts* are God's ability, power, capacity, and force that overrule the natural order by His supernatural power.

The *revelation gifts* are an impartation from the mind of God to the mind of a believer concerning people, places, things, and spirits. It is only a fragment of knowledge from the mind of God.

The *utterance gifts* operate out of a man's spirit and they bring blessing, inspiration, and edification to the church.

CHAPTER 5

Now Concerning Spiritual Gifts: Their Administrations & Operations

> And there are differences of ADMINIS-TRATIONS, but the same Lord. And there are diversities of OPERATIONS, but it is the same God which worketh all in all.
>
> 1 Corinthians 12:5, 6

This is the most important chapter in this introduction to our study of the gifts of the Spirit. We need to ask ourselves this question. How can I be used by the Lord in these marvelous manifestations of His Spirit to minister to the needs of men and women by the supernatural power of the Holy Spirit?

When we think of *"administrations"* our heart's desire should be how can we minister in the gifts? This is the question we all must find the answer to. Our desire should be to be used of God to bring help and hope to hurting people. Who are they? *They are the lost, the least, and the last.*

Webster's New World Dictionary gives this interesting definition concerning "administration." [The administering (of medicine, an oath, etc.)] Another word which means the same thing is *"ministry."* There are different ways to minister the gifts.

One of the gifts of the Spirit is the *gift of healing*. (1 Corinthians 12:9)

The ministry of Jesus shows us that He understood the demonic roots of all sicknesses and diseases and His compassion was for suffering mankind. He sought to seek out and destroy these works in the world.

JESUS MINISTERED BY THE SPIRIT OF THE LORD

Perhaps, the sun was shining brightly this day. There was a smell of freshness and life in the soft breeze that swept the countryside. Jesus was returning from the arid desert with the power of the Spirit surging through His entire being. One thing is for certain, God was getting ready to touch the Earth like never before.

> **And he came to Nazareth, where he had been brought up: and, as his custom was, he went into the synagogue on the sabbath day, and stood up for to read. And there**

> was delivered unto him the book of the prophet Esaias. And when he had opened the book, he found the place where it was written, THE SPIRIT OF THE LORD is upon me, because he hath anointed me to preach the gospel to the poor; he hath sent me to heal the brokenhearted, to preach deliverance to the captives, and recovering of sight to the blind, to set at liberty them that are bruised, to preach the acceptable year of the Lord.
>
> Luke 4:16-19

These were the words that are found in Isaiah 61. Then Jesus did something that caused everyone's attention to be focused on Him that day in the synagogue—He sat down (Luke 4:20).

ONE NIGHT IN A JEWISH SYNAGOGUE

When I attended Bible school, one of my classes was Comparative Religions. We went on a field trip to a Jewish synagogue in Providence, Rhode Island. The rabbi met us and agreed to answer any questions that we may have had. One of the revealing things he mentioned had to do with a verse in what he called our Christian Bible. It was Luke 4:20:

And he closed the book, and he gave it again to the minister, and SAT DOWN. And the eyes of all them that were in the synagogue were fastened on him.

He drew our attention to seats on the platform. He told us one chair was for the cantor (a singer in a synagogue who sings and leads in prayers), there was a chair for the rabbi, and a third chair that was reserved for Messiah. His next words stirred me, he said, "historical tradition says that your Jesus was the only one who ever sat in the Messiah's chair."

The day he sat down was the day He said, *"This day is the scripture fulfilled in your ears."* Luke 4:21 They had known Him as the son of Joseph and now they wondered at what they had just heard and seen. The Master had just declared in the synagogue that He was the fulfillment of the prophecy of Isaiah. He then was challenged by those in Nazareth where he was born.

Later, when He was in Matthew's house for the feast and surrounded by the tax collectors and sinners, the Bible shows us how the Pharisees questioned the disciples as to why Jesus was eating with these people. When Jesus heard them His answer was wonderful;

> **But when Jesus heard that he said unto them, They that be whole need not a physician, but they that are sick.**
> **Matthew 9:12**

The devil tried to stop Him but could not. The people He grew up with did not understand Him. The Pharisees mocked Him. Yet, the Lord understood that a physician was for those who were sick. His mind was not on demonic opposition, the approval of the crowd, or the censure of religion, but instead, He was focused on suffering humanity and bringing healing to deliver them from their sicknesses and diseases.

I believe that this is the work of the entire body of Christ, His church. *Are you willing to pay the price to be used in the gifts of the Spirit?*

Modern day ministry is so far removed from our Master's example that it brings tears to my eyes. There is a generation that denies the power of God; whereas some are just ignorant of the *"administration"* or ministry that brings Christ and His power to bear in these closing days of time.

THE IMPORTANCE OF THE BAPTISM IN THE HOLY SPIRIT TO MINISTER

When Jesus declared that the Spirit of the Lord was upon Him, He also revealed how that Anointing would be administered. The gospel would be preached and miracles of healing and deliverance would come with that Word. This was confirmed by Peter when he preached;

> **How God ANOINTED Jesus of Nazareth with THE HOLY GHOST AND WITH**

POWER: who went about doing good, and HEALING all that were oppressed of the devil; for God was with him.

Acts 10:38

Oh, Hallelujah for Jesus!

When I started preaching we called this kind of ministry a *deliverance ministry*. The gospel was seen first as preaching to the poor, and then healing men and women with broken hearts no matter what the reason, the casting out of devils, and miracles for the blind, deaf, and lame.

The gifts of the Spirit cannot be ministered effectively without that individual being filled with the Spirit. Remember, they are the gifts of the *Spirit*. It is He that causes them to work in the believer. *You cannot do in the flesh what can only be done in the Spirit.*

The word *"gifts"* does not appear in the original text. The Greek word found in 1 Corinthians 12:1 is *"pneumatikos."* The actual rendering of this Scripture is "Now concerning *spirituals* (pneumatikos). That is why the word *"gifts"* is italicized in many translations.

The importance of this is that these *"spirituals"* are not resident in the believer but flow from those things that belong to the Holy Spirit. He gives them to the believer at a *given moment* to minister to the need present. We also learn in this first verse that it is possible that the believer can be *"ignorant"* as to these things of the Spirit and how they operate. The Scripture states;

> "But we have this treasure in earthen vessels, that the excellency of the power may be of God, and NOT OF US."
>
> 2 Corinthians 4:7

God was IN CHRIST, *"reconciling the world unto Himself,"* (2 Corinthians 5:19) but now Christ is in US "the hope of glory." (Colossians 1:27)

HOW JESUS MINISTERED TO INDIVIDUALS

There were thirty-nine people that the Lord dealt with individually in His earthly ministry. It is interesting to me that He did not administer help to them in the same way but He had a special administration just for each of them.

Andrew, He invited to His home. (John 1:39, 40)

Peter, He gave him a new name. (vs 42)

Philip, He found and asked him to follow Him. (vs 43)

Nathanael, He gave a *word of knowledge* to. (vs 47, 48)

Mary, His Mother, He turned the water into wine. (John 2:1-11)

Nicodemus, He challenged to be born again. (John 3:7)

Woman at the well of Samaria, He asked for a gift of water from her. (John 4:7)

A certain nobleman, He healed his son from a distance. (John 4:50)

The impotent man, He gave an instruction to. (John 5:8)

The leper, He touched him. (Matthew 8:3; Mark 1:41; Luke 5:13)

Peter's wife's mother, He took her hand and lifted her up. (Matthew 8:15; Mark 1:31; Luke 4:39)

Matthew, He looked upon him. (Matthew 9:9-13; Mark 2:14-17; Luke 5:27-32)

The man with palsy, He told him to take up his bed. (Matthew 9:2-8; Mark 2:1-12; Luke 5:17-26)

The man with a withered hand, He said stretch out your hand. (Matthew 12:13; Mark 3:5; Luke 6:10)

The centurion, He told him as he had believed it was done. (Matthew 8:13; Luke 7:9)

The widow of Nain, He touched the coffin and spoke life. (Luke 7:14, 15)

The woman with the alabaster box, He forgave her sins. (Luke 7:38)

The Demoniac, He cast the devils into the swine. (Matthew 8:32; Mark 5:13; Luke 8:33)

Jairus, He raised a girl from the dead taking her by her hand. (Matthew 9:25; Mark 5:41)

The woman who had an issue of blood was healed by touching Him. (Matthew 9:20; Mark 5:28, 29)

A woman of Canaan received healing for her daughter by her confession. (Matthew 15:28; Mark 7:29)

A father who had a son with a devil, He rebuked the spirit. (Matthew 17:18; Mark 9:25; Luke 9:42)

The adulteress woman, He wrote in the dirt and questioned her accusers. (John 8:11)

A lawyer, He encouraged to read and obey the Scriptures. (Luke 10:25-28)

Man blind from birth, He spit upon the ground and mixed the clay and anointed the eyes of the blind man and told him to go wash his eyes. (John 9:1-7)

The man who coveted wealth, He instructed to be rich toward God. (Luke 12:21)

Woman with a spirit of infirmity, He saw her, called her, said to her, and laid his hands on her. (Luke 13:13)

Martha, He encouraged her to believe so she could see the glory of God. (John 11:40)

Mary, He justified her gift before others thus honoring her, (John 12:7, 8)

The rich young ruler, He challenged to sell all his goods and give to the poor. (Matthew 19:21; Mark 10:21; Luke 18:22)

Zacchaeus, He ministered salvation to him by going home with him. (Luke 19:9)

Bartimaeus, He had him brought before Him and honored his faith. (Mark 10:52)

The Widow's offering, He taught His disciples how God sees giving. (Mark 10:43; Luke 21:3, 4)

Pilate, Jesus answered him concerning who He was with the Scripture. (John 18:34, 37)

The Thief that was dying, He gave him a place in paradise by

His mercy. (Luke 23:43)

Mary Magdalene, whom He had cast out seven devils, He gave an assignment to take the message of His resurrection to His disciples. (John 20:17, 18)

Cleopas and another man, Jesus taught Scripture to them and fellowshipped with him. (Luke 24:2-31)

Thomas, Jesus ministered to him by allowing him to touch Him. (John 20:27)

Saul of Tarsus, He appeared to him in a bright light and spoke to him. (Acts 9:3-5)

The ministry or *administrations* of the Spirit are plainly seen in how Jesus customized His wonderful saving and healing power for each of these individuals. Their stories found in the New Testament became His story. The key is that He ministered by the power of the Spirit. We see that no two stories are the same and that the Lord has an anointing for each and every one of us.

THE DIFFERENCES BETWEEN ADMINISTRATIONS AND OPERATIONS

Cambridge English Dictionary gives this definition for *administration*: performance of executive duties, the *act* or process of administering something. Oversight of the operation (tasks). [Distinctive varieties of service and ministration.]

The definition given for *operation* is: performance of a practical work or of something involving the practical application of principles or processes. An act or instance, process or manner of functioning. Any action performed "precision, skilled" [of working to accomplish things].

Administrations are simply the *way* that a particular gift of the Spirit is performed, while operations are *which* gift is needed to accomplish that action.

The Amplified Bible gives us this understanding of 1 Corinthians 12:6,

> **And there are distinctive varieties of operation [of working to accomplish things], but it is the same God Who inspires and energizes them all in all.**
>
> **1 Corinthians 12:6 AMPC**

The gifts are special endowments of supernatural energy, and we need these gifts to deal with the devil and to release the wonderful presence and power of the Spirit that blesses the church.

The Bible teaches us that the gifts function differently in each individual. The administration of the *working of miracles* came through Moses' rod (Exodus 14:16), Elijah's mantle (2 Kings 2:8), Samson's physical body (Judges 15:15), the Apostle Paul through the use of cloths he wore (Acts 19:12),

Peter's shadow that released miracles of healing (Acts 5:15), and Christ's healing of a blind man by anointing his eyes with mud (John 9:6).

Matthew chapter 8 shows us four examples of the operation of the gifts of healing, and the way that Jesus administered it. The first example is seen in a leper who came to Christ for healing.

> **And, behold, there came a leper and worshipped him, saying, Lord, if thou wilt, thou canst make me clean.**
>
> **Matthew 8:2**

The Scripture shows us that Jesus touched him and that immediately, his leprosy was cleansed.

Leprosy is a disease of the flesh.

The way that Jesus administered the gifts of healing to him was by placing his hands on the leper.

The second example was a centurion who came to Christ on behalf of his servant. Jesus told the centurion, "I will come and heal your servant," but, the centurion did not feel that he was worthy enough to have Jesus come to his home.

> **The centurion answered and said, Lord, I am not worthy that thou shouldest come under my roof: but SPEAK THE WORD only, and my servant shall be healed.**
>
> **Matthew 8:8**

This was the first time that Jesus had ever seen faith as great as the centurion's. In this case, Jesus administered the operation of the gifts of healing by speaking the Word for healing.

I believe that this is a greater level of faith because that Word can travel distances, accomplish great things without you physically being present, and is a beautiful illustration of God's omnipresence. God is everywhere and we're only *one prayer away from a miracle.*

Palsy is a disease of the nervous system.

Although you cannot touch the nerves with your hands, you can speak a word that gets inside of their body and heals them.

The third example blesses me because it brings honor to a mother. Paul reminds us that if we honor our fathers and mothers, we will have long life on the earth.

> **Honour thy father and mother; which is the first commandment with promise; That it may be well with thee, and thou mayest live long on the earth.**
> **Ephesians 6:2-3**

Peter's wife's mother was at home lying down battling a fever. Jesus went with Peter to his home, and when he saw this dear mother under a physical attack of infirmity, he touched her and she got up.

> **And he TOUCHED her hand, and the fever left her: and she arose, and ministered unto them.**
>
> **Matthew 8:15**

Fever is a disease in your blood.

The *gift of healing* was released to this woman by the laying on of hands.

Our last example is found at the end of the day where Christ is ministering to a great multitude.

> **When the even was come, they brought unto him many that were possessed with devils: and he cast out the spirits with HIS WORD, and healed all that were sick:**
>
> **Matthew 8:16**

Here, we see that some diseases are caused by demon spirits. There are several thoughts concerning *operations* that we should consider because it is important that we understand which gift is needed at the moment.

However, in the eighth chapter of Matthew we are given these four examples and how Christ administered the *operation* of the gifts of healing.

Jesus either laid his hands upon these individuals, or spoke a word that released healing to the people. So we see that the gifts of healing can be released by *administration* through the laying on of hands or the spoken word.

T.L. Osborn, a great missionary evangelist, told me in Chicago, Illinois, that he felt you could minister to more people and see greater numbers healed through *mass prayer*. He had written a book entitled, *Healing En Masse*.

He said, "When you can get all of the people to release their faith at the same time as you preach the Word to them, you will see a *mass prayer* produce *mass miracles*."

In the last example of casting out devils that make the people sick, we should consider how we can operate to bring deliverance to men and women. We have dealt with the fact that there are diversities, or divisions, among these nine gifts. The three divisions of the gifts of the spirit are representative of God restoring man in his spirit, soul (mind), and body.

> **And the very God of peace sanctify you wholly; and I pray God your whole spirit and soul and body be preserved blameless unto the coming of our Lord Jesus Christ. Faithful is he that calleth you, who also will do it.**
> **1 Thessalonians 5:23-24**

When it comes to operating in the gifts of the Spirit, it is important that we understand how God does things.

THREE DEMON SPIRITS

Since the Lord uses the gifts of the Spirit to restore us back to the image of God, what then did the devil use to destroy us spirit, soul, and body?

God works from the inside out, but the devil works from the outside in.

The enemy uses the *"spirit of infirmity"* to try and bring sickness, disease and destruction to the *body*. In Luke chapter 13, we read of a woman who was attacked by a *spirit of infirmity*.

> **And, behold, there was a woman which had a SPIRIT OF INFIRMITY eighteen years, and was bowed together, and could in no wise lift up herself. And when Jesus saw her, he called her to him, and said unto her, Woman, thou art loosed from thine infirmity. And he laid his hands on her: and immediately she was made straight, and glorified God.**
>
> **Luke 13:11-13**

The second spirit that the Bible records is the *spirit of fear*. Fear is an attack upon the mind or soul of an individual. Satan uses the spirit of fear to torment your mind (1 John 4:18). It can come through worry, anxiety, and even panic attacks. However, we are encouraged when we read:

> For God hath not given us the SPIRIT OF FEAR; but of power, and of love, and of a SOUND MIND.
>
> 2 Timothy 1:7

The Apostle John warned us about the *spirit of antichrist*.

> **And every spirit that confesseth not that Jesus Christ is come in the flesh is not of God: and this is that SPIRIT OF ANTICHRIST, whereof ye have heard that it should come; and even now already is it in the world.**
>
> **1 John 4:3**

This certainly goes along with what Paul taught concerning the gifts of the Spirit.

> **Wherefore I give you to understand, that no man speaking by the Spirit of God calleth Jesus accursed: and that no man can say that Jesus is the Lord, but by the Holy Ghost.**
>
> **1 Corinthians 12:3**

It is the Spirit of God speaking out of our spirits as we know that the spirit of man is the candle of the Lord (Proverbs 20:27).

The gifts of the Spirit in operation become a three-fold cord for the full restoration of a man, spirit, soul, and body.

The three-fold cord for operation for a man's body is the *gift of faith, the working of miracles, and gifts of healing*. When you have someone who battles the *spirit of infirmity*, then you know one of these three gifts will bring the desired manifestation.

When you deal with the attack of the *spirit of fear*, there are three gifts that bring a renewing to the mind by the revelation of the mind of God. The three gifts that accomplish this are the *word of wisdom, the word of knowledge, and the discerning of spirits*.

There is a force that opposes the moving of God's Spirit in the world, and that is the *spirit of antichrist*. It is this spirit that is overcome by the mighty anointing of the Holy Spirit in your spirit.

The three gifts that flow out of your spirit are diverse *tongues, interpretation of tongues, and the gift of prophecy*. I look at these three gifts as a direct pipeline from Heaven to Earth. When they operate, they overcome the spirit that is in the world and bring great victory every time.

DIFFERENCES IN OPERATION BUT THE SAME MANIFESTATION

There is an example in the Bible of how two men received the same miracle but by different operations, but they brought the same result to each man.

There was a man in Acts chapter 3, and another man in Acts chapter 14, and they both were crippled from birth.

> And a certain man LAME FROM HIS MOTHER'S WOMB was carried, whom they laid daily at the gate of the temple which is called Beautiful, to ask alms of them that entered into the temple;
>
> Acts 3:2

> And there sat a certain man at Lystra, impotent in his feet, being a CRIPPLE FROM HIS MOTHER'S WOMB, who never had walked:
>
> Acts 14:8

In Acts 3, Peter and John were headed to the temple to pray when they saw this man begging by the gate. There were two gifts that the Apostle Peter operated in that day to bring about the complete restoration of this man who had never walked.

When Peter said, "Look on us," and then commanded him to rise up and walk, we see then that the *gift of faith*, or special faith, was released. When he took him by the hand, the *working of miracles* brought full restoration to his body in that the Bible says he:

> Leaping up stood, and walked, and entered with them into the temple, walking, and leaping, and praising God.
>
> Acts 3:8

In Acts 14, Paul and Barnabas were conducting their first missionary journey, and were in Lystra and Derbe. Here we see a young man crippled from his mother's womb and needing the same miracle as the young man in Acts chapter 3.

However, the operations of the gifts that brought about this same result were different in Acts 14 compared to what the Lord did in Acts 3.

> **The same heard Paul speak: who stedfastly beholding him, and perceiving that he had faith to be healed, Said with a loud voice, Stand upright on thy feet. And he leaped and walked.**
>
> **Acts 14:9-10**

Paul perceived, or had a revelation, that the man had faith to be healed. That would be the *word of knowledge*. It was joined together with the *working of miracles*. The young man received his miracle.

Companion gifts are the working of the Holy Spirit as he uses them severally as he wills. I have always said, "Thank God he is willing!"

These two men were healed. One by the *gift of faith* and the *working of miracles*, and the other the *word of knowledge* and the *working of miracles*. These gifts worked together. Although different operations, they brought about the same result.

Obviously, *diverse kinds of tongues* can operate with the

interpretation of tongues. But now I understood that there are times when different gifts of the Spirit can also work together.

The key to operating in the gifts of the Spirit is that the heart of God's love for mankind must become our passion, as well.

When you and I operate in the gifts, we are manifesting the love of God.

> **. . . faith which worketh by love.**
> **Galatians 5:6**

What is it that gets a Peter and John to stop for a man who has no money and is crippled if it is not the love of God? Why would Paul travel the continent to a people who had never heard the gospel before if it isn't the love of God? Why was it that Jesus commanded his disciples to be filled with the Holy Spirit unless it was his love for the world? Why are we encouraged to desire spiritual gifts and to covet earnestly the best gifts unless it is:

> **. . . because the love of God is shed abroad in our hearts by the Holy Ghost which is given unto us.**
> **Romans 5:5**

The Holy Spirit gives us 1 Corinthians 13 as the great love chapter to balance out the tremendous power of these supernatural gifts.

When Adam stood before God, he received dominion and authority which he eventually lost to that evil one who desired to destroy everything that God created when he made man in his image.

Now, when a man stands before a believer filled with the Spirit and a God-like nature that manifests the gifts of the Spirit, the works of the devil are removed and man is restored.

Again, there are nine gifts of the Spirit, three of which restore the body, three of which restore the mind, and three of which restore and energize the spirit.

How wonderful it is to know that God has a plan to restore us and has given us the means whereby we can achieve total victory in our lives upon the Earth.

When we operate in the gifts of the Spirit and administer them by that same Spirit, we are helping to fulfill God's ultimate plan of redemption. Praise God forevermore!

CHAPTER 6

Now Concerning Spiritual Gifts: Their Purpose

> **But the manifestation of the Spirit is given to every man to profit withal.**
> **1 Corinthians 12:7**

Unless you understand your purpose, you cannot fulfill your destiny. A believer's purpose is defined by the will of God for their life.

> **And cast ye the UNPROFITABLE servant into outer darkness: there shall be weeping and gnashing of teeth.**
> **Matthew 25:30**

The operation of the things of the Spirit in our lives makes us profitable. Jesus indicates that if we're not profitable in spiritual matters, we risk eternal damnation. The Apostle Paul describes the faith of those who are unprofitable as *shipwrecked*.

> **Holding faith, and a good conscience; which some having put away concerning faith have made SHIPWRECK:**
> **1 Timothy 1:19**

Paul writes this to Timothy right after he explains to him the importance of the *gift of prophecy*, which is one of the nine gifts of the Spirit. He encouraged Timothy to operate in the gifts in contrast to those who would not yield to the Spirit.

The purpose of the gifts of the Spirit is to help us to walk in wholeness — spirit, soul, and body. It is God's plan to help us to prosper in life. The Holy Spirit is the source of these gifts. We were made empty that we might be filled.

> **But we have this treasure in earthen vessels, that the excellency of the power may be of God, and not of us.**
> **2 Corinthians 4:7**

THEY AID IN WORLD EVANGELISM

And he said unto them, Go ye into ALL

THE WORLD, and preach the gospel to every creature.

and they went forth, and preached EVERYWHERE, the Lord working with them, and confirming the word WITH SIGNS FOLLOWING. Amen.

Mark 16:15, 20

The Lord led me to put my tent up in the state of Illinois. My wife did not come with me as she was expecting our son. I took that time to get alone with God. Every day, I studied how the gifts of the Spirit operated in the four Gospels.

The sponsoring church had rented a tent from Terra Haute, Indiana and erected it in the city park in Coffeen, Illinois. We used the chairs that the church owned to start the meeting. The more that I studied and demonstrated the gifts of the Spirit in the meeting, the larger the crowds grew. We needed more seats and found chairs that were available in Carlinville at the Assembly of God campground. A local farmer followed me there so we could load the chairs on his truck.

As I drove north, I pulled my car over to watch an Amish family bringing in the harvest in the field next to the road. They had an old-fashioned wagon. The men had scythes to cut down the harvest and the women were wrapping the stalks and putting them on the wagon.

I got back in my car and finished my drive to the campground. It took us about an hour and a half to load the chairs onto the truck and we started our trip back. When we got down by that field where the Amish were working, they were about a quarter of the way into the cut. However, the field on the other side of the road, which hadn't been touched that morning, was now completely harvested. A modern combine was parked in the back of that field.

The Spirit of the Lord spoke to me and said, "Those farmers represent man's efforts to bring in the end-time harvest of souls. They are too slow. The combine represents the gifts of the Spirit and how they will quickly bring in the harvest of souls in the last days."

> **For he will finish the work, and cut it short in righteousness: because a SHORT WORK will the Lord make upon the earth.**
> **Romans 9:28**

The Great Commission is fulfilled by the operation of the gifts of the Spirit. Jesus told His disciples to lay hands on the sick and cast out devils. They would speak with new tongues. These demonstrations are the manifestation of the Holy Spirit.

> **Now when he was in Jerusalem at the passover, in the feast day, MANY BELIEVED in**

> his name, when they saw the MIRACLES which he did.
>
> John 2:23

We can evangelize the world and bring in the end-time harvest of lost souls by allowing the gifts of the Spirit to flow through us as Jesus instructed.

THEY DESTROY DEMONIC STRONGHOLDS

Certain gifts were used to deliver God's children — especially in times of crisis. The *gift of faith* operates in the casting out of devils and gives divine protection.

My wife and I were in Dallas Texas with R.W. Schambach. We became ill after eating in the hotel restaurant. We prayed and the Lord showed me that our waiter had put a powdered detergent in our food. While I was sitting at the table, I told my wife that the waiter was demon possessed never thinking that he would try to poison us. Now we were suffering. We were dizzy, nauseated and felt weak.

We went down to the auditorium for the evening service in this weakened condition. There were about 1,000 people present and my wife sat across from me in another section while I sat with Brother Schambach.

The Lord began to move in that service in a powerful way and the speaker came down off the platform to minister to the people.

The first person he called out was my wife, Bonnie! He

took his finger and drew a circle on her forehead, then, he laid his hands on her and she went down under the power of the Holy Spirit.

Slowly, he turned, looked around the crowd, and walked over to where I was sitting. He instructed me to stand and then did the same thing to me. He drew a circle with his finger on my forehead and then laid hands on me. Down I went! Every symptom left my body and I was healed.

When I got up off of the floor, I went over to my wife as she was sitting up. She said, "Honey, I am healed."

We had never met this preacher, but the Lord led him to my wife and me and we were set free. Amazingly, he picked us out of this crowd and the Lord spared us from that demonic scheme.

Although the devil has evil plans for God's people, the Holy Spirit and these powerful gifts remind us to *"resist the devil, and he will flee from you."* (James 4:7)

THEY CONFIRM GOD'S WORD

> **And they went forth, and preached every where, the Lord working with them, and confirming the word with SIGNS FOLLOWING. Amen.**
>
> **Mark 16:20**

The signs following are a minister's divine credentials. God's ability, power, capacity, and force are unleashed by the Holy Spirit to establish His kingdom upon the Earth. The gospel, followed by signs and wonders, establishes the truth that Jesus is alive.

We see this powerful confirmation in the revival that took place in Samaria.

> **Then Philip went down to the city of Samaria, and preached Christ unto them. And the people with one accord gave heed unto those things which Philip spake, hearing and seeing the miracles which he did.**
> **Acts 8:5, 6**

We see the entire city was stirred by the miraculous confirmation that followed Philip's preaching of the Word.

When Paul went to Ephesus, it was the gifts of the Spirit in operation that confirmed what Paul preached.

> **And God wrought special MIRACLES by the hands of Paul:**
>
> **So mightily grew the WORD OF GOD and prevailed.**
> **Acts 19:11, 20**

May I encourage you who desire to operate in the gifts to give God something to work with. By that I mean, preach the Word. You get what you preach. The Spirit of God and

His Word work together. (1 John 5:8)

T.L. Osborn was preaching in a meeting that my wife and I attended. He told us, "The gospel is simple." Then, he turned to a man seated in a wheelchair and said, "If I wanted you to be healed, I would say 'Jesus heals people who are crippled.' I would say, 'He will help you to get out of that wheelchair.' I would say, 'The Spirit quickens your legs and body.'"

Suddenly, the man stood up out of the wheelchair and started walking. We all jumped to our feet and praised God with him.

Later, we learned that man had been crippled in the Vietnam War and hadn't walked in over twenty years. The gospel is that simple. Preach the Word and God will confirm it.

THEY BUILD UP THE CHURCH

These powerful gifts are not only for the evangelization of the world and the destruction of Satan's power, but also for a supernatural purpose that operates for the believer.

Ephesians 4:12 shows us that ultimately, God uses these gifts through His ministers for the equipping and building up of His saints.

> **For the perfecting of the saints, for the work of the ministry, for the EDIFYING of the body of Christ:**
>
> **Ephesians 4:12**

We see that God uses His men and women with the gifts of the Spirit to bring every believer unto perfection. The word *perfection* also means *maturity*.

One of the examples given is the *gift of tongues* and how it edifies the individual believer. Whereas the gift of *prophecy* builds up the entire church (1 Corinthians 14:4).

Then, in Jude, we read that when we pray in the Spirit, it builds up or edifies our faith.

> **But ye, beloved, BUILDING UP YOURSELVES on your most holy faith, praying in the Holy Ghost,**
>
> **Jude 1:20**

3 ROADBLOCKS TO THE GIFTS OF THE SPIRIT

There are obstacles in the path of every believer who seeks to be used in the gifts of the Spirit. On the Day of Pentecost, 120 believers were gathered together to receive the Holy Spirit. However, after His resurrection, Jesus commanded 500 of them to tarry in Jerusalem to receive the Holy Spirit. I wonder where the other 380 of them were?

There may be a multitude of reasons and even excuses that people give for the lack of manifestations of *spiritual gifts*. But the simple thought is, many in the church are comfortable without them.

We need to realize that without these gifts in manifestation, we can never see the full extent of how God would use us.

ROADBLOCK 1: IGNORANCE

Now concerning spiritual gifts, brethren, I would not have you IGNORANT.
1 Corinthians 12:1

My people are destroyed for LACK OF KNOWLEDGE: because thou hast rejected knowledge, I will also reject thee.
Hosea 4:6

A woman came into the church where I was studying for the revival. She asked, "Is there anyone here who could pray with me?"

The pastor and his wife were in the office and I was in the sanctuary. I saw that she was crying and I asked her what was wrong.

"I've just come from the doctor's office and they've only given me three months to live," she said. This was in July and I quickly calculated that she would die by the fall according to the report. They told her she had cancer.

I looked at her and said, "Jesus heals cancer!"

"He does?" She asked as her crying stopped. "I never knew that He healed cancer. I never even knew that He could still heal."

I gave her some scriptures to think about, told her to come back to the evening service, and told her I would pray for her.

She came back that night and I brought her to the altar where I anointed her with oil and commanded the cancer to leave her body.

I never saw her after that night. I finished the revival and went home. The summer ended and the fall quickly sped by. I found myself at my parent's home for Christmas.

One day, the phone rang and it was my friend who pastored the church where I held that revival.

"Merry Christmas, brother Shuttlesworth," he said. I wished him the same. "I've got a woman here that want's to wish you a Merry Christmas, too," he continued. I thought he meant his wife.

"Brother Shuttlesworth," the voice said. "Do you remember praying for a woman who was dying of cancer this past summer?" I did.

"I've just come from the doctor and they can't find any cancer in my body! I want to thank you for telling me that Jesus is the Healer." That was the best Christmas present that I got that year.

This is why we need to teach on the gifts of the Spirit. This is why we need to demonstrate the gifts of the Spirit. This is why we need to do everything we can to give the world what I call:

Earth's greatest need?

Heaven's greatest answer?
The devil's biggest problem?
These three questions are answered with one name: JESUS!

ROADBLOCK 2: LACK OF DESIRE

> **Follow after charity, and DESIRE spiritual gifts, but rather that ye may prophesy.**
> **1 Corinthians 14:1**

The Holy Spirit had the Apostle Paul show us that the gifts of the Spirit are to be desired. The Spirit of God would not have instructed us to desire the gifts unless He makes them available to every believer.

This brings us to the thought of impartation. Many in the modern-day church do not understand the way that God responds.

> **Delight thyself also in the Lord: and he shall give thee the DESIRES OF THINE HEART.**
> **Psalm 37:4**

There is an interesting thought contained in Paul's writings to the church in Rome as he prepared to travel to see them.

> **For I long to see you, that I may IMPART UNTO YOU SOME SPIRITUAL GIFT, to the end ye may be established;**
> **Romans 1:11**

Paul's desire was to release by impartation, or share with the Romans, these *spiritual gifts*.

Elisha desired the anointing that was upon Elijah and asked for a double portion of Elijah's spirit to come upon him (2 Kings 2:9).

Elijah didn't say, "No. Only I can have the anointing. Only I can be used of God." Instead, Elijah told Elisha the conditions that were required for him to receive an impartation of the anointing that was in his life.

We know by studying the Word of God that Elijah saw eight powerful miracles take place during his ministry. Yet, faithful to God's Word in the mouth of Elijah, we see that Elisha had sixteen miracles and received by this impartation a double-portion anointing.

Throughout the Scripture this is seen clearly. Moses had Joshua. Paul had his Timothy. Desire can be transformed into the fullness of God's plans and purposes for your life. *If you desire to have a gift, then you must sit under that gift.* Jesus taught that the sower sows the Word. The Word is called seed in Mark 4:14. The Bible teaches us that:

> **And God said, Let the earth bring forth grass, the herb yielding seed, and the fruit**

tree yielding fruit after his kind, whose seed is in itself, upon the earth: and it was so.

Genesis 1:11

Elisha poured water on the hands of Elijah (2 Kings 3:11). Joshua stood by Moses and held up his hands and then received the same promise God had given to Moses (Joshua 1:5). Timothy received a spiritual gift from Paul.

You will never obtain that which you do not want. Your desire for spiritual things will bring them to you. Jesus taught:

Blessed are they which do hunger and thirst after righteousness: for they SHALL BE FILLED.

Matthew 5:6

Delight thyself also in the Lord; and he shall give thee the DESIRES of thine heart.

Psalm 37:4

The world refers to those who train us as "mentors." The Bible speaks of "ministry gifts." (Ephesians 4:11) You must have a pastor. You must understand the importance of sitting under the ministry of the five-fold ministry gifts. If you only sit under one of the ministry gifts, you can only be one-fifth perfected. It takes all of the ministry gifts imparting their anointing to bring you to a place of perfection or maturity (Ephesians 4:12).

ROADBLOCK 3: FEAR

> **If a son shall ask bread of any of you that is a father, will he give him a stone? or if he ask a fish, will he for a fish give him a serpent?**
>
> **Or if he shall ask an egg, will he offer him a scorpion?**
>
> **If ye then, being evil, know how to give good gifts unto your children: how much more shall your heavenly Father give the Holy Spirit to them that ask him?**
>
> Luke 11:11-13

When I was a student in Bible school, they assigned us outside ministry. We would preach in churches near the college. My first preaching assignment was in Norwood, Massachusetts.

Pastor Freni oversaw the CCNA church in Norwood. This was a group of Italian people who had come out of the Catholic church and been saved and filled with the Spirit. Their roots go back to the outpouring of the Spirit in Toronto, Canada, at the turn of the century.

I stood to preach in that church on a cold, Sunday morning, but you could tell the people were warm and friendly. When I opened my Bible and got ready to preach, a woman screamed in pain, stood to her feet, and fell over the pew.

Her husband said in broken English, "Her heart, her heart!" He tried to place little, white pills under her tongue. I turned to Pastor Freni to see how he would respond.

"It's your service. Take care of it," he said. Fear like I had never experienced came over me.

I knew that I should pray for her. Then I heard a voice say, "What are you going to do when you pray for her and she dies?!"

Suddenly, the paralysis of fear overtook me. What did I know? I was a nineteen-year-old Bible school student and this was my first preaching assignment.

A strong voice spoke in my spirit and said, "Ask the devil what he's going to do when you pray for her and I heal her."

At that moment, the *gift of faith* rose up in my spirit. I ran back, laid my hands upon her and rebuked the power of death. She blinked her eyes and sat up.

An ambulance came and took her to the hospital. We finished the service and returned to the Bible school.

Brother Freni called the school and asked them to send me back to preach the next Sunday. I thought I had failed miserably and wondered why they'd want me to come back again.

When I got there the next Sunday, an elderly man

stepped out into the foyer, grabbed me, and kissed me on both cheeks. He was speaking Italian and I couldn't understand what he was saying.

Pastor Freni came into the foyer and said, "He's telling you something good. When they took his wife to the hospital after you prayed last Sunday, they examined her and determined that she did not have a heart attack. The next day her doctor came with X-Rays and told her, 'This isn't even the same heart from several years ago. She has a new heart. There's no evidence of heart attacks or heart disease.'"

Fear is one of the roadblocks that the devil uses to keep us from receiving the Holy Spirit and keep us from operating in the gifts of the Spirit.

There are many who have not yielded to the Holy Spirit because they are afraid that somehow the devil will influence them in the supernatural realm.

Yet, Jesus taught that our heavenly Father will give us what we ask for. The things of the Spirit are the good things of God. We understand that,

> **For God hath not given us the spirit of fear; but of power, and of love, and of a sound mind.**
>
> 2 Timothy 1:7

Fear, then, is a hindering spirit and it will attack the believer in the realm of the mind. The things of the Spirit operate out of the spirit of a man. The Holy Spirit uses a natural man for supernatural work. The mind becomes the battlefield where the war is waged.

We are reminded that whatever is born of God overcomes the world (1 John 5:4). So we understand that,

> **The wind bloweth where it listeth, and thou hearest the sound thereof, but canst not tell whence it cometh, and whither it goeth: so is every one that is born of the Spirit.**
>
> **John 3:8**

To receive the Holy Spirit, we must fully surrender to the wind of the Spirit, or the moving of the Spirit. The refreshing of the Spirit is in the wind — or the moving of the Spirit.

When you yield to that moving of the Spirit, there comes a release of joy which removes fear. That joy is birthed out of being born of the Spirit.

> **Therefore with joy shall ye draw water out of the wells of salvation.**
>
> **Isaiah 12:3**

Joy and fear are two different emotions and do not coexist. Fear goes when joy comes!

CHAPTER 7

Now Concerning Spiritual Gifts: Their Divine Nature

There is a great move of God taking place all over the world. The outpouring of God's Spirit is reviving the church, and there is a restoration of all nine gifts of the Spirit to bless humanity.

The gifts of the Spirit are needed to bring the rich presence of God and His power into the believer and universally to His church.

If every believer around the world would begin to operate in the gifts of the Spirit, churches would not be able to hold the results. The last move of God will see a great outpouring and demonstration of the Spirit.

> **And it shall come to pass afterward, that I will pour out my spirit upon all flesh; and your sons and your daughters**

shall prophesy, your old men shall dream dreams, your young men shall see visions:
Joel 2:28

Once again, our nations need this supernatural power. Humanity's every need can be met by the operation of the gifts of the Spirit, and it is how we deal with the devil. This is a powerful statement and even more a powerful opportunity for the church.

God's desire to bless mankind is seen in each of the nine gifts of the Holy Spirit. Their value is seen in their encouragement.

The Apostle Paul's instruction was *"I would not have you to be ignorant" (1 Corinthians 12:1)*. The knowledge of these gifts reveal how *"they profit withal" (1 Corinthians 12:7)*, and we are instructed to *"covet earnestly the best gifts" (1 Corinthians 12:31)*.

You cannot "covet" that which you have no knowledge of. How many teach on the gifts of the Spirit? How many are demonstrating these gifts today? How may we define their meaning? The gifts of the Spirit that are listed by the apostle Paul are nine in number. They are all supernaturally given and you cannot receive them by human endeavor.

Who can explain God? We are looking to Him for the revelation of His nature and how it can help us to overcome every plan of the enemy against us. He has promised, *"And ye shall seek me, and find me, when ye shall SEARCH for me with all your heart" (Jeremiah 29:13)*. What is the first step?

"SEARCH the scriptures; for in them ye think ye have eternal life: and they are they which testify of me" (John 5:39).

His Word gives us this understanding. Paul wrote, *"I would not have you ignorant"* (1 Corinthians 12:1). One marginal rendering says *"without information."* (Thomas Nelson Publishers: KJV, Copyright 1976; Page 1690.) That information comes solely from the Word of God.

The Holy Spirit came from Heaven as God's servant, even as Eliezer was to Abraham. The Holy Spirit brings these gifts to the church and they are a manifestation of Heaven on the Earth. They link us to God's will and purpose. Jesus taught us this truth.

> **Verily I say unto you, whatsoever ye shall bind on earth shall be bound in heaven: and whatsoever ye shall loose on earth shall be loosed in heaven.**
> **Matthew 18:18**

The Spirit of God is always moving through the operation of these gifts. The gifts are the ministry of the Holy Spirit; He is our Divine Helper.

The Greek language of the New Testament refers to the Holy Spirit as the *parakletos, "The One called alongside to help."* All the gifts of the Spirit are for the full restoration of fallen man.

We were created in the image of God. The law of sin and death destroyed man spiritually, mentally, and physically.

Man died spiritually before he died physically. Christ came to identify with fallen man, to do that He emptied Himself of His God-like nature, lived His life as a man (Philippians 2:6-8), and was tempted in all points like we are but without sin. (Hebrews 4:15)

We must understand that the manifestation of the gifts of the Spirit is how the Lord sets us free from sin's dominion and restores us to the image of God.

JESUS WAS TEMPTED IN THE WHOLE MAN

The Gospels teach that man is a spirit. He has a soul which is the mind, will, intellect, and emotions. We live in a body. (1 Thessalonians 5:23)

Jesus was tested in these three realms and overcame the devil's temptation with the Word of God.

1. Jesus was tempted physically. (Body)
Jesus was led by the Holy Spirit into these temptations. This proves temptation is not a sin. The Holy Spirit does not lead us into sin but delivers us from evil.

When Jesus fasted it speaks of His union with fallen man, *"And in those days he did eat nothing: and when they were ended, he afterward HUNGERED" (Luke 4:2).*

When *Adam ate* in disobedience, sin and death entered into our world (Genesis 2:17; Romans 5:12). *Christ did not eat* in obedience to the Spirit's leading, which brought Him to the cross where He reversed the curse of sin and death (Galatians 3:13).

2. Jesus was tempted spiritually. (Spirit)

"If thou wilt worship me, all shall be thine." (Luke 4:7) We are reminded that *"God is a Spirit; and they that worship him must worship him in spirit and in truth." (John 4:24)*

Tests reveal the true nature of an individual and Jesus knew that, *"No man can serve two masters." (Matthew 6:24)* When we are tested, it is to reveal to us what we have in us. God already knows what is in man. (John 2:25) He wants you and me to know what we are dealing with in our lives.

3. Jesus was tempted mentally. (Mind, will, intellect and emotions)

The Devil's challenge to Christ was, *"if you are God's Son then throw yourself off of the pinnacle of the temple then angels will watch over you" (Luke 4:9-12)*. The devil uses pride in people to keep them from being used of God.

> **Let no man beguile you of your reward in a voluntary humility and worshipping of angels, intruding into those things which he hath not seen, vainly puffed up by his fleshly mind,**
> **Colossians 2:18**

All three of these temptations were real. Satan could not offer the world to Christ unless he had dominion over it.

Paul taught, *"in whom the god of this world hath blinded the minds of them which believe not, lest the light of the glorious gos-*

pel of Christ, who is the image of God, should shine unto them." *(2 Corinthians 4:4)* Satan is seen as the god of this world after the fall of man. He is referred to as *"the prince of the power of the air," (Ephesians 2:2).*

When Jesus overcame these temptations in the wilderness He renewed us from the inside out. This was Paul's prayer:

> **And the very God of peace sanctify you wholly; and I pray God your whole spirit and soul and body be preserved blameless unto the coming of our Lord Jesus Christ.**
> **1 Thessalonians 5:23**

The light of Christ brings forth a change in the believer. That light is the image of God shining in us. We are transformed into that image by the operation of the gifts. *"But the manifestation of the Spirit is given to every man to profit withal." 1 Corinthians 12:7*

The word *"manifestation"* is translated from the Greek word *phanerosis*. It means a *"shining forth."* The light of the gospel preached activates the nine gifts of the Spirit. Jesus is the source of that light. Jesus said, *"I am the light of the world: he that followeth me shall not walk in darkness, but shall have the light of life."* (John 8:12)

As the gifts of the Spirit operate in the life of a believer, Christ shines forth through their manifestation. The revelation gifts are like headlights on a car. The further you go, the more you see. The battery powers the headlights that shine through their lenses. The Holy Spirit is that power and through the *"manifestations"* of the gifts He brings the ultimate restoration to all mankind, "spirit, soul, and body."

We find that these nine gifts fall into three categories. What the Scripture refers to as *"diversities."* (1 Corinthians 12:4) these three divisions of the nine gifts reveal the nature of God.

1. God's Omniscience is seen in the revelation gifts.
The three *revelation gifts* are a *word of wisdom, word of knowledge, and or discerning of spirits*. They help us to THINK like God. God is ALL KNOWING and His knowledge is unfathomable and inexhaustible. He reveals by the Spirit to a believer a part of that knowledge from His mind.

> **For now we see through a glass, darkly; but then face to face: now I KNOW IN PART; but then shall I know even as also I am known.**
> **1 Corinthians 13:12**

The revelation gifts are limited information from the unlimited knowledge of God, and given to the mind of the believer in part from the mind of God. Thank God for the part we have.

2. God's Omnipotence is felt in the power gifts.

The three power gifts are faith, *working of miracles*, and the *gift of healing*. They help us to ACT like God. God, Who is the All-powerful One, brings mastery over demons, sicknesses, and diseases and executes authority over the natural world with supernatural power. He gives by the Spirit power to the believer to overcome.

> "And Jesus came and spake unto them, saying, All power is given unto me in heaven and in earth."
> **Matthew 28:18**

These gifts are for our body's health and strength.

3. God's Omnipresence is heard in the utterance gifts.

The three utterance gifts are *prophecy, divers tongues, and interpretation of tongues*. They help us to TALK like God.

He speaks by the Spirit through the believer Divine words of faith, encouragement, and instruction. The believer may operate in the utterance gifts anywhere because God is everywhere.

David said, *"If I ascend up into heaven, thou art there: if I make my bed in hell, behold, thou art there." (Psalm 139:8)* God is with the believer anywhere and everywhere speaking by the Holy Spirit. These gifts are for our spirit.

The Spirit of God works in the spirit of a believer. The definition of each of these gifts provides a guide line to the rules which govern them and the understanding of their activation through God's great love to help people and reverse the curse of the devil who seeks to destroy the image of God in man. These gifts are an impartation of God's mind, power, and voice in part to help us to conform to His image and glory.

The revelation gifts are for your mind or soul.

The power gifts are for your physical body.

The utterance gifts are for your spirit.

Our full potential as the *"manifest sons" (Romans 8:19)* of God is restored by the operation of the gifts of the Spirit. It was this God-like nature in man that Christ spoke of in *John 10:34* when He answered the religious leaders that challenged Him. *"Is it not written in your law, I said, ye are gods?"*

Although this has been a problem text for some, it is better understood as the gifts of the Spirit operating in godly men and women. When they challenged Jesus He responded by saying *"believe the works" John 10:38* He appealed to the miracles and gifts of healing as the vindication of the restoration of God in a believer.

LESTER SUMRALL AND THE PACK OF ALASKAN WOLVES

I personally heard brother Sumrall tell this story. He was ministering in Alaska and decided that he would go for a walk and take pictures of the beautiful scenery. Alaska is crowned with beauty from the Denali mountain range to the shores of the Bering Sea.

He was walking along the edge of the woods, when suddenly, a pack of wolves came running out of the forest. They surrounded him snapping and snarling at his heels.

Brother Sumrall had been working on a book called, *Lester Sumrall Unveils Dominion*. The Lord instructed him to use that dominion and take authority over those wolves. He said, *"I didn't have a gun and just a camera that day but I found out I had something greater."*

He testified that he spoke to the wolves and commanded them to go back into the woods. They spun around and went away! God's nature works through man if we allow Him.

The gifts are seen and understood as "manifestations" and become the spiritual definition of the *"new creature in Christ Jesus"* 2 Corinthians 5:17 operating with the divine credentials of God's confirmation.

As the gifts of the Spirit manifest in your life, they guarantee that you are being led by the Spirit into a successful life of blessing. You will make a supernatural impact upon your generation.

DOWNLOAD OUR APP.

Search "Ted Shuttlesworth" in the Apple App Store or the Google Play Store.

DO YOU NEED PRAYER?
Call us today: 1-888-323-2484
Visit us online: www.tedshuttlesworth.com

WHAT I'VE LEARNED ABOUT THE BLESSING

God's Blessing will take you from financial failure to a good life. Throughout the years I have proven that the biblical principles of increase work.

I gave God one dollar when I was eighteen, and He gave me a ministry to touch the World. I have learned that The Blessing is greater than the curse and the Lord cannot fail.

You can be the one that changes your family's financial future. There are many of God's Children who are living far below their potential. When you understand the connection between prosperity and the winning of lost souls and faithfully operate in these Biblical principles then you can expect to receive God's Blessing.

shop.tedshuttlesworth.com

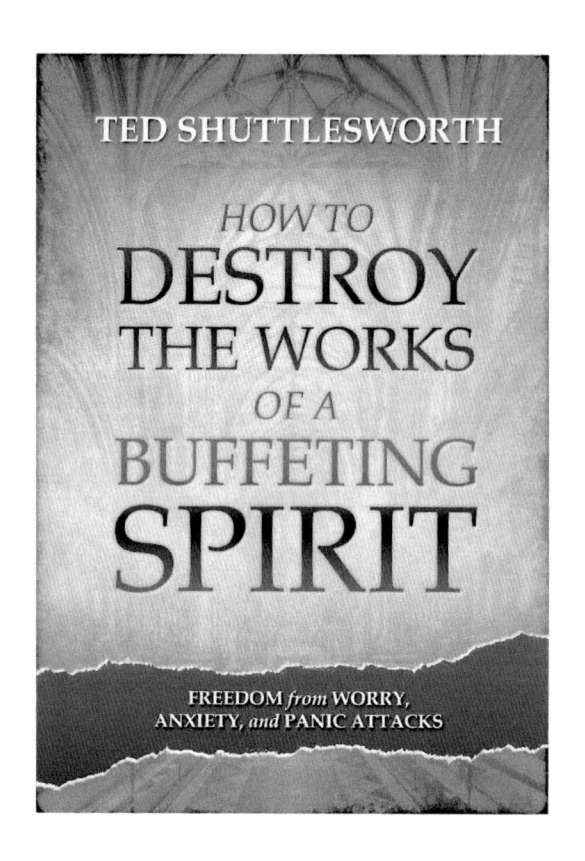

HOW TO DESTROY THE WORKS OF A BUFFETING SPIRIT

Today we are witnessing unrest and trouble which are affecting the nations of the world. There are many who are fearful because of the uncertainty of the times.

Anxiety disorders are the most common mental illness in the United States affecting 40 million adults 18 years of age and older according to the National Institute of Mental Health.

There are many people who are managing anxiety with medications, psychiatrists, and even hypnosis. What if these attacks were being caused by demon spirits? Learn what the Bible has to say about how to be free from worry, fear, anxiety, and panic attacks!

shop.tedshuttlesworth.com

HOW TO RECEIVE YOUR HEALING

It is God's will for you to be healed. Faith for healing comes from the hearing of God's Word.

"But so much the more went there a fame abroad of him: and great multitudes came together to hear, and to be healed by him of their infirmities." Luke 5:15

Here is a step-by-step, scriptural plan that will help you to receive your personal healing from Jesus Christ. A great faith-building book for those who have been chronically ill.

shop.tedshuttlesworth.com

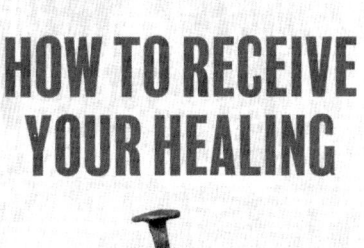